"Oh, how we fill our lives with things we don't need and often don't even want! In *My Year of Buying Nothing*, Lee Simpson is always entertaining as she shares her own discoveries of the stuff that clutters our days without making them better, and is then trucked off to the landfill unloved. Through her own experiences, helped by family and friends, she reminds us that it's not having it all that makes us happy, it's appreciating what we do have. It's a very timely message and Lee Simpson actually makes it fun to hear." – Rick Wolfe, Advisor to Changing Businesses at PostStone

"There are lots of books telling us to be more environmentally conscious consumers. There are lots of books telling us how to spend less money. However, there are not lots of books that take these topics and discuss them in such an original, useful, charming and reader-oriented manner. This is a great read with great insights." – Alan C. Middleton. PhD., Assistant Professor of Marketing, Schulich School of Business, York University

■ Lee Simpson

My
Year
of
Buying
Nothing

■ Wood Lake

Editor: Mike Schwartzentruber
Designer: Robert MacDonald
Proofreader: Dianne Greenslade

Library and Archives Canada Cataloguing in Publication
Simpson, Lee, 1951-, author
My year of buying nothing / Lee Simpson.
Issued in print and electronic formats.
ISBN 978-1-77064-801-2 (paperback). ISBN 978-1-77064-802-9 (html)
1. Simpson, Lee, 1951-. 2. Simplicity. 3. Alternative lifestyles.
4. Sustainable living. 5. Grocery shopping. I. Title.
BJ1496.S54 2015   179'.9   C2015-904956-3   C2015-904957-1

ISBN 978-1-77064-801-2

Published by Wood Lake Publishing Inc.
485 Beaver Lake Road, Kelowna, BC, Canada, V4V 1S5
www.woodlake.com | 250.766.2778

We acknowledge the financial support of the Government of Canada. Nous
reconnaissons l'appui financier du gouvernement du Canada. Wood Lake Publishing
acknowledges the financial support of the Province of British Columbia through the
Book Publishing Tax Credit.

At Wood Lake Publishing, we practice what we publish, being guided by a concern
for fairness, justice, and equal opportunity in all of our relationships with employees
and customers. Wood Lake Publishing is committed to caring for the environment
and all creation. Wood Lake Publishing recycles and reuses, and encourages readers
to do the same. Books are printed on 100% post-consumer recycled paper, whenever possible. A percentage of all profit is donated to charitable organizations.

Printed in Canada
Printing 10 9 8 7 6 5 4 3 2

■ Table of Contents

■ Dedication

THIS BOOK IS DEDICATED IN A SPIRIT OF RADICAL GRATITUDE
to the inspiration of Mary Jo Leddy,
Canadian activist, theologian, and woman of faith,
without whom much that is good in my life
and those of so many others
simply would never have happened.

■ How We Got from There to Here and Some Words of Thanks

YOU MAY WONDER HOW A PERSONAL VOW AND PRIVATE CONVER-SATION WITH CLOSE FAMILY MEMBERS in the last week of December of 2013 morphed into your reading these words.

As I was doing my planning, I mentioned to a couple of people what I was up to. Over New Year's lunch, my friend Gail, who was teaching me to knit, gave me a lovely little black-and-white notebook to record the travails and triumphs of the year ahead. That's when I decided that if it went well, I might be able to write a short essay for *The United Church Observer* magazine. Knowing enough of the advance planning that goes into producing a year's worth of issues, I suggested I could write my reflection up for the December issue, calculating that if things did not work out, I could let the assigning editor know well in advance. As a regular contributor to the publication, I figured they might be interested in a 1,000-word piece for the back page and sent off an email to that effect.

And that's how my debut as a blogger and now author of a book came about. David Wilson, editor-publisher of *The United Church Observer*, a trusted friend and former colleague, got right back to me to propose 500 words. Every two weeks! I trust I am capturing the gist of his pitch back to my pitch: "Readers don't want to hear how smug you feel after succeeding, Lee; they want to watch you squirm all year!"

Well, who could resist? I talked the idea over with my husband who already had a blog for professional reasons and encouraged me to go for it. And I signed on. The first blog came out in mid-January, when I was still working out the basics. It was fully supported by the magazine's public relations team who showed me how to promote on Facebook. (I was already chatting there with some folks about life lessons and dog videos.)The team also taught me how to Tweet, a new and increasingly valuable skill.

The response was swift, in much larger numbers than we initially expected, and mostly supportive though there were detractors. That tall-poppy syndrome kicks in whenever something new appears and hasn't yet been tested in public. But then the media caught on and the interviews started. Luckily, my media training from way back kicked in and I again became comfortable talking on radio and television, and doing print interviews. Later in the year, I participated in a video-documentary on my Year of Buying Nothing (YBN), as it came to be known. And I got the call from the publishers of this book that resulted in the words you are reading now.

If you asked me now how I feel about all this attention, I admit that it has turned out well. I have lost count of how many people have come up to me to tell me they are trying a year, a month, or even a week of buying nothing but edibles. I know what they do not yet realize as they make their initial plans: it will change their buying patterns forever. This year has changed my life and I am not talking about the blog and the book. The publicity has been and gone, but the discipline of discerning for every buying decision *what I want versus what I truly need* will remain part of my planning, budgeting, and ultimate purchasing for the rest of my life.

Even if you are not thinking of attempting this yourself, come with me on a stroll through 12 months of challenge and acquisition – not of *stuff*, never again for me the unquestioning acquisition of stuff – but acquisition of *knowledge*. Hey, it's recyclable!

* * *

I WOULD LIKE TO ACKNOWLEDGE THE CONTRIBUTIONS OF OTHERS TO MY YBN, foremost my family: my beloved husband, Paul; "Great Kate," Alex, Franklin, and Milo on this coast; Georgia and Jack, Dad and Muriel on the other coast; and Jo in the middle. None of you ever lost your patience or sense of humour with my project and you were all so very inventive!

My friends were supportive and giving, too, (often literally): Kearney and Barbara, Joy, Lee, Kathy, Kathie, Chris and Christine, Diane, Susan and Tom, Wendy, Syd and Sandy, Al and Gladi, Kirsten, Sharon, Marilou, Ross and Pat, Jarrod, Gail, Jim and Donna, Elizabeth and Richard, and the HBC gang. Many of you will find yourselves in these pages.

From the congregational side (which is also my workplace), I am especially grateful to the Gift-Pack Gals(!), the Spirit Study gang, and the members of Trinity United Church and St. Paul's United Church of Mahone Bay and Stonehurst/Blue Rocks respectively, who showed such interest in this project.

For her long friendship with our family and her teaching gifts, which are not limited to the kitchen, I am endlessly indebted for life-lessons received from Lil Hurst.

My special thanks for professional assistance go to David Wilson, Kevin Spurgaitis, Jocelyn Bell, Dayo Keftense, Rick Wolfe, and Sara Jewell. Gratitude goes to Mike Schwartzentruber, editor, who will have to check these words, in addition to the other 69,000. Looking forward to more than virtual coffee someday, Mike. You made this so much easier!

■ Introduction

HAVE YOU WANDERED THROUGH THE TOY AISLES AT YOUR LO-
CAL BIG BOX STORE RECENTLY? You probably wouldn't think
that this would be the backdrop for a life-changing epiphany.
But it was for me. Right there, in the midst of the puzzles and
the puppets, just weeks before Christmas, somewhere between
the pink-fluffy-crystal-princess section and the camouflage-
monster-truck-superhero row, I hit the wall. That would be the
wall of consumer overload. I had a revelation: the purchase of
a toy for a two-year-old could be likened to enrolling our offspring into a cult. A cult of gender-stereotyped, manufactured-
offshore, corporately-branded, non-recyclable, plastic *stuff*.
Stuff guaranteed to be rendered obsolete at the checkout counter. I was buying my favourite child a ticket to a dangerous and
addictive lifestyle.

This eye-opening moment was made ten times worse by the
fact that I helped invent this nightmare. As publisher of
Chatelaine magazine during the 1980s and '90s, I had overseen
the heady days of women's magazines. The largest issues ever
were published then, circulation was at an all-time high, and so
were newsstand sales: those big, fat editions with their high-
gloss covers sold well. The resultant healthy profits yielded a
vast quantity of excellent journalism and I remain proud of the
pioneering work of the editors with whom I worked. But my
primary role as senior executive was to ensure that a maximum
number of advertising pages got sold so that we could pay for all
those good writers, photographers, investigative journalists, and
creators of colourful food, décor, and beauty features.

Coercing ad dollars out of cosmetic, packaged-goods, pharmaceutical and automotive manufacturers and into our pages
where we could surround them with a comfortable environment
of suitable copy – that was the game. Being both glib and genuinely sure of my goals, I was good at it. Understanding their
marketing strategies and supporting their aims, I wheedled
chunks of cash out of corporate pockets and back I strode, in

my stylish heels, to our editorial team, urging them to come up with even more lavishly beautiful shots and seductive words about recipes, style, travel, and home fashion.

I was part of the machine that made women want to have the latest lip gloss, yearn for a programmable coffee maker and need *that* particular T-shirt. None of which is indefensible. We were, after all, the first generation in significant numbers to earn our own direct bank deposits as equal working partners. We surely had also earned the right to spend those wages as we wanted, once household contributions were made.

So where does this go off the rails, ethically? M-m-m, probably around the time the communications industry started to think about the marketing wisdom of the multiplier effect of smart branding. If that budget lipstick looks good on you, just wait until you see this pricey mascara from the same line. If you adored the design of that coffee maker, you will *love* the crepe maker that they also offer. Never mind that it never occurred to you before to make French pancakes at home in enough quantity to warrant such an appliance; think how professional it will look! And that T-shirt in red? Wow, it comes in four more colours: better get them all now, while they have your size. The affluent '80s were a time of broad shoulder pads and thick skins when it came to elegant indulgence.

On the path to excess, everything is paved by smart marketers who have your number. And I, among others, gave it to them. I was part of the data analysis and market research conglomerate that helped the consumer predators know your weaknesses and exploit them mercilessly.

How fitting, then, that my punishment should be meted out in the toy display of my local Walmart! There I stood, lengthy Christmas list firmly in hand, credit card at the ready, struck dumb by the realization that I, among legions, had been an author of the book of doom that threatens our planet.

We are drowning in that stuff – breakable, unnecessary, imported, useless, and non-biodegradable. And here I was, eager to invite someone I love to take Step One on the road to consumer perdition. I was ready to buy (and wrap up in cartoon-character-themed, non-recyclable paper) that first installment in a lifetime of overconsumption of nasty plastic junk. *I* was purchasing the thing that would make *him* want to buy the accompanying DVD, dress the doll, get the matching vehicle, and eat the sugary cereal that comes in the shape of the same dumb character. I was about to initiate the acquisition of the endless proliferation of poorly made, uninspired dreck that follows on after you take Step One. In the name of familial love, I was about to do this!

It had been a long time since I had small children on my Christmas list. I was brought up in an era of wooden puzzles with animal shapes, modelling clay, and Tonka building sets. Buying for our own children, now grown, had naturally included Barbie and Lego, but I had no idea just how much the selling of toys and dolls had changed. I was shocked to discover those items had now morphed into shelf after shelf of never-ending related accessories. There are few things you can conjure up as brand extensions for that cartoon character or movie princess, not already on offer. Sadder than anything, *nothing is left to the imagination*: literally, children are not required to utilize their rich potential for fantasy to interact with this generation of toys. If you suggest that the average 5-year-old might want to play superhero, they will not raid the linen closet for a cape, they want you to buy one – the right one – the one for their own particular favourite from television, DVD, or online video. Lego is no longer assorted plastic interlocking pieces: it comes in kits to make a specific thing. If you want to make a different thing, you have to buy another kit. Parents in our time were cautioned to avoid demanding that little hands crayon within the lines for fear it might stifle artistic creativity. The games likely to evolve from these shelves are *intended* to be predictable, stultifying the otherwise limitless imaginings of children's minds for creative play.

Beyond the plastic fragility of most toys, ensuring they don't easily survive the rough and tumble of the playground but must be handled carefully, preferably indoors, there is some truly troubling gender stereotyping. Girls get pink and frilly; boys get black and, more distressing yet, *military camouflage*. Yikes! How did this happen? According to the *American Economic Journal*, the presence of women in MBA programs increased from 4% in 1970 to 43% in 2006. How did the reality of equal enrolment in MBA programs (of which, as one of only three women in a class of 64 back in the '80s, I had been so proud) result in this? How on earth do these educated women and the liberated young men who graduate with them, find themselves designing and marketing toys, condone blushy-rose, froth-infested, disturbingly sexualized dopey dolls?

Recent studies from the Toy Industry Association, which collects international data, agree that most items for sale in the world's toy aisles were provided by cheap labour from China, Indonesia, Mexico, and Viet Nam: by 2007, China alone accounted for 80% of the toys sold. Those trucks and tiaras may sport familiar American brand names from movies and theme parks, but they are mass-produced under unknown labour conditions and transported at great cost to the environment. And the recall rate for toys and dolls that have proved injurious or even lethal, due to shoddy manufacturing practices and layers of toxic paint, continues to cause concern.

And that was my moment of enlightenment. Right there, leaning on my empty cart, I recalled a slogan from the early days of the feminist movement: "If you are not part of the solution, you are part of the problem." My previous life as a useful cog in the marketing machine had led to this precise point.

I couldn't undo what I had done. But I could stop contributing to a system that enslaved our grandchildren in this never-ending pattern of buy-and-discard. So I went home, without a Christmas gift for my best little pal, but with the beginning of a plan.

I recalled a radio interview from some months earlier: two young singles in Calgary, roommates Geoffrey Szuszkiewicz and Julie Phillips, were partway through a year of not purchasing anything they didn't absolutely have to buy. Their story was inspirational. But they were at a very different stage of life, without the obligations and expectations of family and work that accompany middle age. Could I do this? Could I expand my boycott of pre-fab toys to a larger vista?

I sat down at my laptop and started to draft out some rules for myself. I knew I would have to bring my husband into this. Imagining that discussion meant preparing answers for his questions. I also needed to think through the impact on our extended family. I had to develop guidelines that permitted me to continue work that meant a lot to me.

This is a good a place to share something of myself. I am a mature (ahem!) woman, a mother of one and grandmother to two, married and living in a rural area, 20 minutes from daughter and her family. Our move to this part of the country was made a few years back, in line with new goals after many decades of a big-city, two-career lifestyle. We love the country life. We are not too far from a major urban centre, where my husband teaches university and we are close to our family.

As mentioned, I was publisher and vice-president in a major publishing company for many years. When our daughter was small, I was a proud member of the league of career superwomen who planned to have it all, and I came darn close. My husband worked in policing, first teaching at the police academy, later developing training programs and consulting on executive policing issues all across the country. We were deeply engaged in our work but had a great network of support for bringing up our child. My mother resided with us for 20 years and my in-laws lived around the corner: we had backup for every childcare dilemma. And the marriage-saving luxury of taking a walk in the evening without having to book a sitter.

Spoiled? Perhaps, but our lives revolved around family. We had less glamourous hobbies than many of my high-powered business colleagues. While they golfed, we camped. Their Mediterranean cruises were our road trips to visit friends my husband had made in his work; cops are great hosts and we were privileged to be part of a circle that kept us grounded. And I *needed* to be reminded that my job was a privileged one. My work allowed me to meet three prime ministers and countless celebrities, among them Gordon Lightfoot, Roberta Bondar, Diana Krall, and Margaret Atwood. Pierre Elliot Trudeau kissed my hand in a salute to my just-announced pregnancy. This was heady stuff!

In contrast to the high-powered celebrity glamour was the inspiring community of down-to-earth folk I encountered in our church, a congregation deeply involved in social justice and community activism. I was not then a hands-on outreach worker; my contribution was to fill the gift basket that was raffled off to pay the bills for the local homeless shelter. But we were regular attendees and dutiful members, supporting Christmas pageants and helping with coffee hour.

That was Sunday morning. Sunday afternoons were for family: Scrabble games and big-batch cooking so that we could eat meals together at home on weeknights, too. This was the rule, even if my husband and I had to head back to our desks once our daughter was asleep. This was how we kept our feet on the ground and heads out of the clouds despite the seductions of the corporate life.

Things changed completely just before the millennium. After 25 years in the advertising and publishing industry, I was, if not burnt-out, at least toast, close to fried. That top-speed, high-pressure time had begun when I was so young, not only the first woman in my executive role, but the youngest person ever. When I contemplated another 20 years of daily meetings, monthly deadlines, quarterly re-forecasts and annual budget presentations, it seemed suffocating, not stimulating. Our company had been taken over by another and the clear path to greater executive power was no longer open to me. Mostly, I was bored and restless. There must be something more…

And there was, and is! I became more directly involved with that church. I traded my duties as church school liaison and chair of social events for Worship Committee and Board Member to get a closer look at what was involved in ministry. It's a longer story, but suffice it to say by 2005 I was an ordained minister in The United Church of Canada and happily served in congregational ministry, both urban and rural, and later as part of a renewal of our denominational magazine, *The United Church Observer*.

And what does any of this have to do with my Year of Buying Nothing (YBN)? I present this brief snapshot of where I was in life when I undertook my YBN so you will better understand some of the items that made it onto the list of ground rules and what got omitted, as well as my reasons for wanting to commit to this self-inflicted deprivation.

If I had to summarize my reasons, it would be as follows:

1) to express a private *mea culpa* for a career focussed on making women want things they don't need
2) to learn how to leave a smaller footprint on our struggling environment
3) to prove to my own family's young people (who are way ahead of me on this) that I can be a gentler user of our earth's resources
4) to see just how much I would save, and
5) to prove to myself that I could change my habits.

Along the way, I learned a great deal. The chapters that follow are anchored by my sharing of education. I had a very fuzzy idea of exactly how much environmental damage I was committing with my careless buying and usage habits. If I were sitting in your living room right now, I would look you in the eye and say: "Changing your ways is so much easier than you think!"

It is also fun and I hope to provide you with a few grins of recognition, smiles of accomplishment, and outright belly-laughs at my folly as your read about my year.

In preparing for this adventure, I tried to be as organized as possible, examining budget records from previous years and doing a room-by-room survey of potential needs. I completed a thorough inventory of what we had on hand. And then I set down my ground rules.

Here, then is the pledge I came up with for the period beginning January 1 and ending on December 31. For a year, I will buy nothing that I cannot eat. Specifically, that means not purchasing

- clothing
- furniture
- appliances
- antiques or second-hand items
- cosmetics or toiletries
- paper or plastic grocery products
- books or magazines
- craft supplies
- plant/garden supplies not related to edibles, and even then attempting trades where possible
- gifts or greeting cards or stationery
- computers or techno gadgets

There were exceptions that I built into the guidelines, anticipating my husband's questions; after all this was *my* quest and not his and it was not my purpose to make his life difficult:

- toilet paper
- regular household expenses to be paid: Internet, electricity, heat (though we tried to stick to wood stove, not furnace), taxes, insurance, snowplowing of our driveway
- DVD and video rentals
- usual vet bills for our dogs
- prescription medications should they become necessary
- charitable donations based on the previous year's pattern

Planned compromises to the rules were the result of discussions with family:

- one meal out a week in a restaurant (*my* year was not to become my *husband's/friends'* deprivation), restaurant to be local, not chain, and meal to be modest
- coffee from my local vendor limited to three times per week

■ transportation to be kept to essentials: utilizing public transport in town (did I mention I was once Queen of the Cabs?) or in a family car that was making the trip anyway. Full disclosure – I do not drive and never have and will address how this impacted my YBN later in this book.

■ three haircuts a year (this reduced from customary nine)

■ contact lenses replaced on usual schedule

■ vacuum cleaner to be replaced (When the year began, ours had just died and we were borrowing to keep up with hair from two Cairn terriers; this was not optional unless we planned to give up breathing!)

■ gifts would be accepted but, if asked, specifying services, rather than "stuff": a pedicure or an extra trip to the hairdresser.

My husband and I debated the subject of family travel and came up with the following compromise:

■ My usual annual jaunt to see my elderly father on the other side of the country would be allowed – reasoning that missing this might be something I would regret more than any pride I might take in a successful YBN.

■ Our family camp vacation, four adults, one child, three dogs, one car, no Internet, TVs, radios, newspapers – this may not sound like a good time to some, but we have been doing this multi-generational week-long trip for 31 years now and that was non-negotiable for everyone.

These were the rules I recorded. You may not be surprised to hear that they would get revisited during the next 365 days.

The question I was asked most frequently in the following months was a variation on this: "Did you stockpile in advance?" (Or its more accusatory twin: "You must have pantry-loaded for months before you started this!") The short answer is, "No, I didn't have to." Let me explain.

I did an inventory of what we had on hand and was a little shocked. Had I been planning for a nuclear winter? The world's longest grocery store strike? Nope, just being your average over-acquisitive consumer. I was ready for those events of deprivation because I bought things "just in case." Things like laundry detergent, four different brands of large-size, eco-friendly suds for my HE washing machine. For two people – you get the picture. I was ready for a dirty-clothes emergency of epic proportions; World Cup soccer played in an ocean of mud wouldn't have phased my level of preparedness.

Feeling confident, I moved on to the bathroom. Armed with common sense and a desire to go on being married, I recognized that giving up toilet paper was not an option. I was taken aback to see only three boxes of facial tissues. I went in search of that stack of underused cloth hankies. They would do. Between us, my husband and I had amassed a wardrobe of shampoos. My lingerie drawers were stocked with way too many fancy hand soaps for a lifetime of grubby paws (and way too few decent pairs of cotton underpants, as it turned out, but that is a tale for a later chapter). My bathroom drawers yielded stocks of forgotten eyeliners, lipsticks and glosses, and, more pertinently, five partially used deodorants, plus one bottle of my favourite bubble bath: "Hey, why was this the year nobody gave me more!" I grumbled. Later I would weep over that omission.

After the tour around the upstairs areas of our home, I checked out the kitchen cupboards and the cleaning supply shelves. On the cleanser front, I had a few of my old standbys, plus a very large box of baking soda and the elbow grease my grandmother had advised was a cleaner's best pal.

Giving up buying paper and plastic products I acknowledged as a challenge. For example, I had become reliant on the Swiffer system for floor care. To continue that regimen would require replacing those many-and-increasingly offered disposable portions – not just for my YBN. And those replacements parts I did not have in quantity.

In the kitchen, I had become accustomed to the ease of re-sealable plastic bags; they are tidy for packing away leftovers, freezing planned-overs, or making packed lunches. I had only half of a 50-pack of the sandwich size, which previously might have done for a couple of months; I was down to four of any other size. And then, there was my old pal, the paper towel dispenser. Half a roll and no backup! How was I going to do the things I was accustomed to doing in my kitchen? Pat veggies dry before stir-frying, pick up small spills, cook bacon in the microwave?

I avoided panic by reminding myself sternly that there was life in our grandmothers' kitchens before disposable paper products became prolific. Paper towels were not mass-produced until the 1930s and my own mother resisted them as an unnecessary luxury until the '70s. I comforted myself; I had a ragbag and I knew how to use it! Plastic wrap was also getting low, but I vowed to survive. Mercifully, I had taken recent advantage of a special on aluminum foil and had 150 feet.

In short, I was in business! It was late December and I was eager for the rigours that New Year's Day would bring. Little did I know what lay ahead.

■ A Word about the Structure of this Book

IF YOU READ THE INTRODUCTION, YOU WILL RECOGNIZE THE "ARCHITECTURE" OF THIS BOOK. When planning my YBN, I had to take note of what I wanted to accomplish over the year, make some basic rules and guidelines, and take inventory of what was on hand to help me get to the end of the 12-month period, sane, still married, and not completely friendless.

The plan for this book was similar. Instead of days, I had a budgeted number of words to put in front of you, the reader. I didn't mind the thought of making a few friends along the way, but I was happy to settle for stirring some controversy. At the same time, I *did* need some guidelines to help me get to the end of the book with the resources of ideas I wanted to share, without overdoing it. So a plan for both my YBN and this book about it seemed called for.

The plan was simple: I tried to subdivide the experiences I had and the information I had to share under a very ancient rubric: Animal, Vegetable, and Mineral. To illustrate, under "Animal," you will find collected all those activities that bring out the "beast" or "animal" in us, for example, adorning ourselves, whether it be with clothing or cosmetics, taking care of our manes… Similarly, with "Vegetable" I discuss all things edible and potable; and, in "Mineral," I tackle energy conservation – think planes, trains and automobiles, plus home heating and the like, cleaning and appliances, and entertainment.

There is a fourth classification, "Spirit," for those for whom a spiritual perspective on these activities would be of interest. Those who do not share this point of view are welcome to skip Chapter 10.

■ Part I

Animal

**(as in, those things that appeal to
our "animal" nature)**

■ Chapter 1

Clothing

THIS CHAPTER DEALS WITH THE ISSUE OF HOW TO KEEP YOUR-SELF FROM GOING NAKED AND CHILLY SHOULD YOU UNDERTAKE A YEAR OF BUYING NOTHING (YBN). If I do my job, it will also inspire you to be a better steward of your closet under any circumstances. It deals frankly, unblushingly, and almost exclusively with references to female clothing. Although I have tried to add in male equivalencies wherever I have personal knowledge, I have not walked a mile in your brogues, Gents. Emotionally speaking, this is an unvarnished memoir of *my* YBN; some experiences do *not* jump gender barriers and I apologize in advance to readers who are seeking that aspect. Maybe this will inspire some men out there to give up buying for a while, record the challenges, and share how they managed their own solutions.

■ How the state of our closets challenges our state of mind
When I began my YBN, I had precisely 31 garments hanging in my bedroom closet. In the front hall, I kept an additional four items: two spring or fall jackets, one raincoat, and one parka. In total then, 35 items all together, not counting the PJs, lingerie, hats and other bits and pieces that dwell in drawers. Those things *do* count, believe me, but more about that later.

Let's be clear. Although I was never what might be termed a "follower of fashion," this does not represent my wardrobe at its most abundant. As a senior executive in the communications industry, I had a substantial number of changes of the dress-for-success uniform: two-piece suit and blouse or shirt. I, unlike most of the world, happily had beauty and fashion advisors who helped me dress appropriately. Because I lean toward a classic style and was a bit of a hoarder, those excellent clothing items had transitioned from corporate lunches to church halls quite well. But that was then...

In the months prior to my YBN (and not yet having the notion I would undertake this project) I had done a thorough clear out, with the idea in mind that I would catch the sales in January of the new year. The downsizing had been tactical and deliberate: as a retiree from the workaday world of pumps, pantyhose, and dignified two-piece suits, I wanted to shift everything that smacked of the office and speakers' circuit right out of my life and into that of someone who needed a decent wardrobe to wear to work. Good riddance, literally!

Me? I was going to hang out in the garden, walk the dogs, write a bit, and play with our new grandson. I needed jeans (I had three pair); corduroy pants (four); two pairs of "good" trousers; one black skirt and two blazers, one black and one citron. I had a dress that could be worn on its own or paired with a jacket for fancy dinners or funerals. That left 18 somewhat tired tops in assorted colours, with a predictable preponderance of white, black, and blue-stripes on a white background. As well, I had assorted T-shirts and turtlenecks lurking in my dresser.

Perfect, right? Yep, it would have been the complete package had it not been for an unexpected development. Early in my YBN, a colleague became ill and I got called into a ministry position in a neighbouring church and needed a polished and professional look for three or four days a week. And there I was, committed to buying absolutely nothing to put on my back (or front).

A little background. There is a fashion among memoir writers that places a whack of blame for what goes wrong in adult lives on the "Monster Mom." When I mess up, I don't have that excuse as I did not have that mother. Mine was a delightful person, witty, with enlightened opinions and an abundance of common sense. She was also a beautiful woman, slim and elegant, who did occasional stints as a "hand" and runway model. I proudly accompanied her to see one of her saunters out on a brightly lit stage. She was modelling a sweater design by textile artist Kaffe

Fassett, in front of an audience of 1,500. She was calm and confident, and she was 82 at the time.

My sister and my daughter both inherited this easy-going sense of style and the lean look; they can wear anything and look great. I have seen my dear sibling, heading for a hike in the mountains near her home, grab an old parka from the closet of a son, and mash a toque on top, her face bare of makeup. She looked marvellous. And she is past 50. Looking great has no "best-before date" for women with style.

My own daughter has so little interest in conventional fashion that she asked her father and me to help her decide on her wedding dress *the day before* the big event. She had two choices: a traditional organza prom dress uncovered in a local second-hand store, or an eyelet-cotton sundress (borrowed from a bridesmaid) leftover from a garden party. We selected the latter, though frankly she looked smashing in the crinolined-finery of the former. And when she walked that aisle, she was stunning.

Oddball assemblages of used finery on my family seem stylishly deliberate. Me? Not so much. On me, they look like oddball assemblages. I need to plot my look. I am my father's child in looks. Also, I adore food and love to cook. I wrestle with my weight and have to dress around it. I love bright colours, both in my home and on my back. But I recognize that neither age nor my choice of career favour year-round, bouncy yellow-and-scarlet combos. Looking stylish does not come naturally to me, though I can still pull it off when I expend the effort. Making that effort can be a pleasure when preparing to go out for a fancy meal with my husband. But it is simply *not* a priority on a daily basis. I need grab-and-go that ends up looking dignified.

This is an explanatory prelude to sharing the impact of that sudden re-entry to the workaday world. My YBN situation forced me to really "work" the limited number of items I had. As a result, I developed more fashion savvy than anytime previously in my life. When you have less, you must make it do more. This is a skill that contemporary dressers rarely have to exercise, but one our grandmothers understood well.

■ A word about closet-indigestion

Unless you live in a cave, you must have spotted those massive walk-in closets in the media. In advertising, décor magazines and real estate shows, the impression is created that potential homeowners may want to exercise the option of opening a retail clothing outlet in their "master suite." Maybe you, like me, have asked yourself, do those walk-in extravaganzas actually exist beyond the mega-homes of celebrities? I thought the phenomenon presented a distorted version of reality, so I did some homework on what goes on behind closed *closet* doors in your average neighbourhood boudoir.

According to *ThreadFlip*, a U.S.-based Internet company, the average adult closet holds between 90 and 135 items at any given time. This is up from approximately 22 items 30 years ago, says the UK's *Daily Mail*.

Women have two to three times as many individual garments as their male counterparts. But we do have other habits in common. *ThreadFlip* tells us that, for both genders, as much as 51% of the things on those hangers do not get worn within a 12-month period. The *Daily Mail* suggests that one out of every five clothing items purchased will *never* be worn and the heavy-use period even for favourites lasts about a month. I doubt that trends are different in North America.

Let us cast our eyes downwards to the floor of those closets for the shoe stats. In 1986, we were shocked by Imelda Marcos' collection of over 1,200 pairs of shoes. How could she wear all those? Well, she didn't. But we are not in a position to throw stones. Of the average 20 pairs found in a woman's closet today (12 for a man), only one-quarter is in active rotation. Some shoes languish forever as they are too uncomfortable for us to jam our toes into even once, after the torrid love affair in the shoe store.

The fleeting attraction of fashionable-but-excruciating footwear is the stuff of sitcom episodes, and also of our daily lives. The number of shoes owned by the average person is going up every year at a rate that shows no sign of slowing down. I could get all snarky and blame *Sex in the City*, but that's because I am not into shoes and never have been. I have never owned more than 15 pairs at a time and that includes hiking boots and snow gear. I lean toward comfort when it comes to feet, but I admit to the occasional lapse, and I do "get" the passion that others have for glorious shoe-wear. Admittedly, they do something for your look and for your ego. My mother had tiny, fine-boned feet and loved elegant high-heeled confections. And I am a compulsive polisher of my husband's shoes, and admiring of all those lovely tooled leather brogues and moccasins that well-shod gentlemen sport. I have owned Italian Ferragamo loafers back in the day, and I do know the bliss of slipping one's foot into an exquisitely made shoe – just don't add a three-inch spike, thank you.

Now back to that rack of clothes hanging above our fetish inducing foot-garb.

■ How I got from January to December without showing up naked

Before I undertook my YBN, it had been my intention to buy a new "good" coat. I had been forced to ditch my beloved calf-length, black down overcoat the previous spring. The annual cold-wash-and-tumble-dry left it leaking tiny feathers like snow all over our laundry room. I was sad because that coat was my pal on city streets, at church events, and on the speakers' circuit for a decade. Then, post my YBN decision, replacing this coat was no longer going to be an option.

This still wouldn't have been an issue except that the remaining parka was a pretty-but-brilliant shade of blue. I purchased it originally because I loved the colour and I justified it: at least I couldn't be lost in a snowdrift when cross-country skiing with more athletic friends. Since it was all I had (and warm), I wore it early in the year for a media interview during the first wave of YBN publicity. When the accompanying photographer suggested we head outdoors for a few shots in the snow, I didn't think twice about it, fully expecting to see the resultant human interest feature reproduced on page 12, in yawn-inducing black and white. Two days later, there I was, on the front page of a major newspaper, sporting the second most famous blue coat (Leonard Cohen owns the first) in the land. (This is the only way I am every going to find myself in the same sentence as my troubadour hero, so I thought I'd slip that in.)

I had become instantly recognizable as "that woman who isn't buying anything." Most people were very kind and their remarks supportive. However, some mistake any degree of celebrity as an invitation to poke and pry. In the following months, I was stopped repeatedly in the supermarket as folks checked what was in my grocery cart. One woman prodded the items already in the basket quite aggressively when I had turned my head long enough to do a price check on dried lentils. "I see you've got a lot of those expensive organics," she sniffed judgmentally and flounced off.

Most of the time, I welcomed the notice the coat received. The staff where I banked was very kind and counted down the months along with me. The librarians who worked the desk where we pick up our books were interested and supportive. That coat turned out to be a calling card most of the time, and I came to appreciate that it opened up conversations about my anti-acquisition-of-stuff campaign. It was a blessing in its own in-your-face way.

But back to how I managed to dress myself beyond the warmth of that coat.

There I was, all dressed down but suddenly with somewhere to go – somewhere I had to show up looking decent! It had become evident that the friendly neighbourhood congregation would need assistance beyond the original assignment and likely through to the end of the year. So the big question became, "What will I wear?"

This is not the frivolous, looks-obsessed folly it may at first seem. It is important for members of the clergy, male or female, to look the part. Your pastor is supposed to be the non-anxious presence in whatever situation he or she may find themselves. That might be a hospital bedside, a seniors' residence, a funeral, a wedding reception. Then there are the day-to-day meetings, from the minister's-study-cozy to the agenda-driven boardroom. You have to dress appropriately, but in this – of all callings – you don't want to be spending too much time fussing about it, because to do so would be downright unseemly!

I am sympathetic to the philosophy of Barak Obama, who reputedly wears exactly the same look every day to avoid "decision fatigue." He is concentrated on doing the most he can for his country. But Obama has an unlimited budget to purchase the components of his presidential look. I was stuck with a mishmash of leftovers and a commitment not to buy a single stitch of fabric.

Depending on the tone of the church you represent, you are expected to appear in the pulpit either in robes (white or black with a stole), in a traditional "servant-shirt" with clerical collar, or in business-like civvies. Luckily for me, this congregation appreciated their minister's "robing up," that is, donning the ankle-length white or black gown and the seasonally appropriate stole. I had those things tucked away in a box downstairs and, bless their capacious folds, they covered a multitude of sartorial sins. Great! That took care of two hours of the workweek.

Most contemporary clergy in our denomination keep the "servant-shirt" with white ("dog") collar for nursing home and hospital visits, where the people on whom we call are reassured by seeing this traditional garb. I had two of those shirts.

But other than that, I was thrown back on a couple of pairs of "decent" dress pants, those tired leftover-from-my past blouses, and two blazers. The baggy corduroy pants, the faded blue jeans that I thought would be my daily dress? They got kicked to the back of the rack in favour of the final few remainders of my office life.

Boy, did those items get a work out! Remembering the advice of TV *fashionistas*, I stuck to basic solids and accessorized the heck out of everything to make it fresh and attractive for each event. I had silk, wool, and cotton scarves draped over every frayed collar. I rolled the sleeves of blouses with tired cuffs and paired them with sweaters. The button box got raided to refresh an exhausted white blouse with an array of mismatched novelty toggles. A beige shirt with a mustard stain got topped with a chocolate brown T-shirt and a jaunty belt. (Please, God, let the smiles that particular look evoked be because of my "jauntiness.") Earrings and bright cotton squares that hadn't seen daylight in a decade made a "look" out of that jacket over a series of contrasting sleeveless summer tops – even in December! With all this subterfuge, I felt confident that when pulpit time switched to coffee hour, I was able to whip off the robes to reveal something tidy, if not "fashion forward."

A note about those wardrobe warriors that got the greatest use: they were generally of excellent quality. Two quick illustrations. The first is a white cotton tuck-pleat blouse. It was a Valentine's Day present from my husband. A gift from him, because I had admired it in an Irish import store that closed in 2008, so I reckon that blouse is at least five years older than that. The citron-coloured summer-weight jacket I mentioned is a Klaus Steilmann, and I bought the expensive piece in celebration of ditching the maternity look I had sported all the previous season. Our daughter is now 32; you do the math. I had that boxy short sleeved beauty re-lined two years ago and the tailor admired the craftsmanship.

My point is that quality of workmanship is worth investing in, whether you save up and buy new, or have a good eye for discards at church rummage sales, or thrift and consignment stores. Clean lines and classic design have "wearability" well beyond the fashionable must-have of any season.

■ Pounding the beat without spending a penny

Shoes were a bit more of a challenge. I owned and had in regular rotation (besides useless-for-the-purpose sandals, hiking boots, and runners) a pair of dark grey ballet flats, brown lace-up walking shoes, and a very good pair of red moccasins. As to this latter indulgence, a wise fashion editor once advised that no woman's wardrobe is complete without a pair of red shoes;

they can add punch and style savvy to any look when worn with panache. This is one of those life-truths worth passing on.

Any basic footwear wardrobe should also include good black pumps and flats. I took inventory. My then-current and only pair of pumps were an unwise bargain purchase that caused pain with every mincing step. The sole of my black moccasins had (de)parted from their "snake-skin" uppers some months before. This was not their first separation and the shoe repair expert suggested that the marriage of top and bottom was not salvageable. Out they went, leaving me just this side of shoeless.

When life serves up red shoes, toast to the crimson toes and celebrate! I wore red lipstick and red Tees and red earrings and red brooches and red scarves (not all at the same time). I trust I was creating the impression that the shoes were my signature and the rest of my garb members of the supporting cast. If not, I don't need to know. The slightly more discreet ballet flats peeked out from under black dress pants at more formal events. Somehow, I got through the year with the dignity of my calling intact.

■ My secret strategy

A few words about underwear. I am a well-endowed woman. By the time I graduated high school, though slim of frame, I sported a C-cup bra. The years and having a child have pushed that to a double-D. With good posture, this is no drawback to dressing well. I like my body and always have and I make no apologies for this. Thanks to a mother who, though very different in body-type herself, was always supportive, I enjoy a healthy self-image. I have also always loved good lingerie.

When I first left the town where I grew up for an extended vacation in the big city, I was determined to buy something for myself that celebrated the occasion. It turned out to be an investment that marked the beginning of a lifelong habit. Not for me the purchases my travel-mates were making in patchouli-scented boutiques: flowing Indian cotton, leather vests, and Nehru-collared jackets. Around the corner from where we were couch-surfing, I had spied an elegant store with a window full of lace and satin and a discreet calligraphy sign indicating that they custom-made bras. I was fitted and picked up my finery a week later; Black Watch tartan with black lace, panties, and garter belt to match. (For those readers I just lost, that belt was how we kept our stockings up before pantyhose.) I still have that bra, and many of the other beautiful-yet-sturdy lingerie confections that followed. Well-fitting underwear is your best fashion friend, and if it's pretty and makes you feel like a million bucks, it is well worth it. Carefully washed by hand using good, pure soap and hung to dry, a well-made undergarment has staying power.

A word about the psychological lift of knowing you look good under that suit, within that smock, or beneath that uniform: I sat around enough testosterone-scented boardrooms that I developed strategies to beat the blues of being the only woman in the place. When I offered an idea and it was ignored, only to subsequently find the exact same notion voiced by "one of the guys" and greeted as tactical manna from executive heaven, I could have settled for quietly seething. When I found myself exiled from the male golf/football bonding around the coffee urn, I could have given in to feeling left out. But I had a secret weapon. That excellent underwear got me through many a bad meeting. I pictured the sad-sacks around me in their threadbare boxers and droopy grey briefs. It's a variation on the old "picture your audience naked" idea, only better. Judging by all the careful adjusting that goes on of those thousand-dollar suits, I'm pretty sure most of the executive male bodies they drape do not look like the sexy models in the Calvin Klein ads. Filling in the imaginary details put a secret smile on my face. Hey, it got me through the day.

I once accompanied two very close friends on a girls-only escape-from-winter holiday. It had been a challenging year for all three of us. Sarah's husband had died of cancer a few months previously, Annie was recovering from a hysterectomy, and I had left my job and was due back at school after many years away. We spent a lot of time debating which room to take in our rented beachside condo, and unpacking our colourful, island-getaway wardrobes. I was sharing a closet with Sarah, who watched in open disbelief as I unearthed from tissue and carefully hung five matching pairs of bras and panties (which I thought quite modest as we would be gone for a whole week). She'd stowed her one black/one white bra and assorted pants in a drawer within 30 seconds and there I was still fiddling with frills. "Do you always travel like that?" she finally blurted out. I explained a little of my lifelong love affair and admitted that had my husband been with me, there would have been even more and prettier pieces hanging there, just waiting for the right moment.

She looked at me oddly: "So you really think there's a link between the longevity of your relationship and your lingerie?"

"Absolutely!" I enthused. (I am thinking we'd already had a cocktail?) "It keeps things lively."

There was a long pause: "So what you're suggesting is that Tony might still be alive if I had worn racier underwear?"

I can still feel myself going pale when I recall this moment of horror at what she might have read into my words, then I noticed her grin. Sarah, who has a wicked sense of humour and is my role model in all the big transitions of life, was, once again, teasing me.

That week the three of us laughed and cried and danced. We learned how to make salsa from scratch and how to cook artichokes. We swam and painted our toenails and explored where turtles hang out. But mostly we teased each other back to life, with my underwear proclivities providing hours of giggles.

Good lingerie, whether daytime support or nighttime pretty, has other uses and definitely adds to sexual self-confidence. Although I have been married for a very long time now, I was not born this way. Back in my dating days, it was a very good feeling to know that should the occasion arise, I could meet the challenge. I know your mother told you to always wear clean undies in case you were in an accident, but trust me, she knew of other reasons. And as a happily married woman, I will just add that partners *do* pay attention to such things. A little mystery is a useful thing to keep in marriage. You may be surprised to know how much attention the person who loves you pays to what you wear under your workaday duds. It is useful even in (or perhaps *especially* in) a long relationship to insert a pause between fully dressed and stark naked. If that happens to be pretty or sexy or racy from time to time, all the better for both of you.

Whether your personal taste runs to satin fripperies or pure cotton and sporty underthings, it is well to keep them in good shape. (More on how later.) Before I advanced into my YBN, I had intended to replace some of my more tired basic cotton panties, which come three-to-a-pack and are so useful under jeans. (It's not *all* lace and froth in my underworld, either.) But, alas, there was no January sale for me. My "good" underwear sets stood up very well. My cotton and more utilitarian bras had a rough ride; droopy and elastic-exposed, they barely made it through. When visiting my sister, I found myself surreptitiously unpacking when she wasn't looking so she wouldn't feel sorry for me. But a needle and thread helped a lot and that's something we can talk about.

■ Every "dud" deserves a second chance

One of the suggestions I heard most frequently (usually by once-sympathetic friends listening to me go on and on about that puffy blue coat) was why I couldn't just go to a second-hand store to get a decent black replacement. I must admit, I pondered over this one for quite a while when setting the rules.

I am a fan of thrift stores. We have a chain here called *Guy's Frenchys Family Clothing*, which even rated an essay in the *The New Yorker*, written by Calvin Trillin no less. They feature giant bins of gently used clothing that are refilled as often as hourly. It is a bonding ritual among the locals that I have been happy to join in, spending a day with pals both male and female, going from branch to branch, refuelling with coffee and doughnuts along the way. I bought my daughter's maternity wardrobe that way. *Frenchys* are discreet about their sources, but reveal they come from the U.S. When my husband and I lived in Italy, the teachers in the school where we were employed taught me to scour the carts in the weekly markets for bargains in pre-owned jackets, pants, and sweaters. A lot of the clothing was of very high quality indeed. It was clear that someone was on the look-out for them in Germany and France, and as far away as the U.K., judging by the labels.

In truth, second-hand clothing is big business globally. When you do a closet-cleanse, you are setting those items out on a tour of the world you only wish you could afford. Yes, they may get no further than the for-profit *Value Village* in the next town, but they *could* be off to Ghana, where as much as 60% of all clothing purchased is imported from sources suspiciously like your dresser drawers.

The ethics of what *should* happen to used clothing are complex and I would urge the truly committed to attend to online discussions, because this is a developing issue. The bottom line in an environmental sense is that it may seem more socially responsible to donate your used T-shirt than to dump it in the landfill. But from the perspective of respecting manufacturers and retailers of fledgling indigenous clothing businesses in countries such as Ghana, for example, the effect of "dumping" cheap hoodies and brightly coloured skirts is clearly nothing short of disastrous. And the dumpers may surprise you. Even Oxfam was previously on the receiving end of criticism regarding their practices. (They have since amended their policies.) It is a dilemma.

So when it comes time for you to pass it on, be generous, by all means, but be informed. Check out the signage on your local supermarket parking lot drop-box as not all are created equal. If the details of where the donated items are headed are not entirely clear, you may find you are donating to a for-profit retailer. This is your business, but you should be aware.

Value Village is a lot of fun to shop at for Halloween. They are retailers like most others, in business to make a buck. They buy from a lot of charities including the Canadian Diabetes Association. The CDA is imaginative enough to pick up used clothing: very useful if you are helping sort out the wardrobe of a deceased loved one. They use the proceeds of their sales to fund research and diabetes education. Both The Salvation Army and Goodwill Industries accept donations from you for sale in their local outlets. Goodwill is diligent about ensuring that as much as possible of what is donated is put on display at good prices after being repaired by paid employees. The training that is received is valuable to those who may then find employment beyond the charity's workshop. Leftovers from sales are inevitable; turns out *nobody* wants lime green corduroys this year. The money that is earned by the sales of those leave-behinds at The Salvation Army may be given back as vouchers for families in need. At Goodwill Industries it is used to fund employee training of the disabled and new Canadians.

Only you can decide how directly you need to control the afterlife of your velour leggings and cotton button-downs. Personally, I try to donate as *locally* as possible. Both our daughter and my oldest friend work with disadvantaged youth trying to make a start in the world. There is a branch of the international registered charity *Dress for Success* in our area and that is where the balance of my aforementioned office wear ended up. If my husband had items to pass along, I would check out the male equivalent in town.

I like to support the goal of helping appropriately outfit those who are trying to enter or re-enter the workforce because of my personal links, but there are innumerable good causes. For more casual wear, including gently used nightwear, children's clothing, bed linens and towels, try a women's shelter. Sportswear, warm jackets, hats, mitts and snow gear? An Out-of-the-Cold or other program for the homeless will likely take donations directly. Be a good "sort-sport," though, and call in advance of your delivery and do not just dump on the doorstep of these organizations; they have their volunteer sorting schedule and may be short of storage.

Then again, the local church, synagogue, or mosque is a wonderful way to ensure you know exactly where your donation will end up; sometimes with quite humourous results. I am both a giver and a receiver at rummage sales and have often had a quiet smile of recognition at seeing that pencil skirt I bought on a mistaken whim looking fabulous on a fellow parishioner. On the other hand, I suspect a silk scarf I purchased at a church bazaar two years ago is equally recognizable to the UCW president. I don't give a darn; that is as it should be.

Don't forget the possibilities of your more adventuresome garb finding a new life in a dress-up box for the daycare, camp, or local little theatre. This is particularly true for things like wedding and prom dresses, motorcycle gear, cowboy boots, or other western gear. All items of this kind are useful to the imaginations of the creative. And every nursery and playschool I have ever visited had the need for quick cover-ups for little ones' efforts at the easel, a wonderful way for men's shirts to have a second life.

Even closer to home are friends and family. It remains the custom for infants' and children's clothes to be passed along to other young parents. *There should be no shame in this for any age.* My mother thought it sensible to offer to the woman who helped keep our house clean a bag of clothes for her kids, items outgrown by my sister or me. I often saw my mum tuck in a pretty skirt for Fatima herself, or a shirt for the husband of our family friend.

Yes, I know that makes some want to gag at the picture of one individual playing Lady Bountiful at the expense of the pride of another. Get over yourself. This is good common sense and prudent stewardship of our environment. Nobody had to make extra trips in the car, there are no ethical issues for developing nations, and people have wearable garments to put on.

I have made it a practice in the recent past to "gift" family members and friends with things they admired from my wardrobe – mostly costume jewellery, but also the occasional scarf or hat. My step-mum has been a grand source of nearly new T-shirts for my own summer wear (we share a bust size). A few years ago, a good friend who doesn't have money to spare, lost a lot of weight. I had things that I knew would fit her (because I *hadn't* lost weight); so to help her celebrate, I made up an outfit from my closet. It was with some trepidation that I initially broached the subject, but she was delighted. I recall very happily seeing her in a blue chambray skirt and peasant top that looked adorable on her newly slim physique.

Later, when my beloved brother-in-law died, our daughter was without the requisite dress slacks in a strange city with hours to go before the funeral. A good pal of mine initially loaned her a pair after my suggestion that they (being of a similar build) might get together. They may have been a generation apart, but quality black wool trousers are a standard item. My friend later gave them to our daughter who probably still keeps them on hand for the next inevitable event. How is any of this wrong? It makes no sense to buy new every time the need arises. Sisters and university roommates share clothes. We all can.

At the end of the day, however, there remains the globally threatening nightmare of too much fabric. My reasoning in banning myself from *all* purchases except food for the year, including second-hand, was that there is too much stuff in the world and an endless pipeline of more flooding in. Let's be brutally honest here. When we take that tired blouse off the hanger to give it away, it is *because we are about to buy another one*, not because the other blouses all got fat and needed more room. Or maybe we already bought that floral chemise (and the matching/contrasting pants) and simply have to jettison one to cram in the next. It's all wrong. And crafty retailing marketers make sure it will never seem enough.

Even if you are buying second-hand, someone, somewhere is *already* preparing to replace the original, apparently in multiple copies. Someone is planting cotton on a piece of land where life-giving trees were cut down so they could sow that crop. Someone is tending those plants, liberally soaking them with pesticide before they reap the poisoned harvest. Someone is sending those bales of cotton by smelly diesel truck to be manufactured into cloth. Someone is dyeing that cotton with toxic chemicals and the runoff is polluting a river. Someone, probably far too young, is cutting and sewing that fabric into a blouse in a dangerously overcrowded firetrap of a factory. Someone is packing it onto skids made of pine from another clear-cut ex-forest. Someone is readying that crate for an oil-guzzling tanker ride across our once-pristine oceans. Someone is unloading that crate and trucking it across another 1,000 kilometres of highway, emitting carbon all the way. And someone is unpacking and loading it onto a store rack, all prepped and ready to become another cute top, for me. How many of those someones truly labour in safe conditions? How many are reimbursed appropriately for their labour? How many of those acts of violence on our earth are tallied as part of the true cost of that cute top?

You see, I couldn't in all conscience set in action that chain of events during my YBN, a year designed to break that cycle for me. I'd like to say that I never participated in that chain of events or will again, but that would be a lie. But I *did* learn one incontrovertible lesson: if ever there was a place where "less is more," your closet may be it.

■ Tales of mystery: "The ethics of ermine" and "Lessons in leather"

Recently, a friend inherited two fur coats from an elderly aunt. Being savvy about fur, she did not want to wear them or turn them into throws, and had an aversion to seeing them end up on the street. Her feeling was that putting them on display in any sense would suggest that it was okay for others to buy and wear *new* fur coats, thus perpetuating an industry that has a deservedly poor reputation. For my friend, who lives in Scotland, there did not seem to be an easy end to this dilemma. Eventually, she did find a theatre company that would use them in plays depicting a time before awareness of the issues involved in wearing fur became broadly known.

If you have an animal pelt coat to unload, you may be equally challenged. Second-hand stores and consignment shops may decline your donation because they are fearful of PETA protests. Charities do not want to saddle their impoverished clientele with a problem coat, however warm. The only surefire way to avoid the issue of fur disposal is not to buy one in the first place and to refuse any inheritance that includes such an item. And that goes for fur trim, too. There is a marketer right here in Canada that uses coyote fur pelts as a signature accessory on their down jackets. Coyotes are not well-loved around these parts, but they do not deserve to die terrible deaths in under-inspected leghold traps so that I can have a prestigious parka.

Two words about natural fibres: fur, bad; leather, good. Right? But wait. Does that make sense? Obtaining leather is not like sheep-shearing. An animal died so that we could be covered and shod. But we don't think about animal hides the same way we do about animal pelts. I have witnessed protesters of the fur industry striding up and down in fashionable boots, footwear I am certain is not made of vinyl.

So given that a mere 40 years ago, wearing fur was the norm, whether neck-to-calf or as an adornment of a winter outfit, how soon will it be before I start hiding my hiking boots even when not protesting? And I am reliably informed that leather, unlike fur, being treated with chemicals so it doesn't rot on your feet, will not meekly disappear into your compost. So you will, like my Scottish pal, have to work long and hard to discard that once-prized, now-offensive item.

Now, I am not introducing this to send you scurrying to your shoe rack to rid it of all animal hide and donate while you still can. I share this to illustrate the complexities of the developing challenges of our times. With knowledge comes responsibility. I am not a vegetarian. I am not opposed to the humane rearing of animals for the purpose of feeding humans. My own family raises chickens for eggs and owns cattle for meat. I would prefer it if I could believe that all animals are decently treated and given an end without undue stress. Indeed, I work quite diligently to ensure this is the case for family consumption (more about this in the section on food). Naturally, I would also like to think that the animal's carcass was subsequently completely used up, snout-to-tail and that the hides were included in that list of planned usage. But information on leather sources is much harder to come by. The abuse of cattle in India and China, where the balance of modern shoe leather comes from, is a matter of documented evidence. This issue is not going away and is not solvable by you and me, all on our lonesome. But we can use information and reason to try to decide our personal line in the shifting ethical sands.

What is clear to me is that I don't *need* to own fur. Leather is a more recent dilemma. I am less certain that pleather really works in hiking boots. I own a pair of genuine Italian leather ones, only eight years old now, which for comfortable hiking means nicely worn-in. I treat them with care and they should see me out. That leaves the remainder of the footwear I will purchase to mull over. I have a source of footwear that I like and trust as far as manufacture is concerned (and given factory conditions for mass-made shoes of any kind, this should be a concern). San Antonio Shoes (aka SAS), Texas, makes sturdy leather footwear on site at its factory in that state. They have labour practices of which they are proud and you can visit to see your shoes being made. Sadly, their website is less forthcoming about the source of that leather. Some manufacturers are starting to be advocates of sustainability and animal-humanity. Increasingly, I suspect this information will be available online. My take? I will be very cautious about any leather shoe purchases in future and keep them to absolute necessities.

But let's face it: we are all making these purchasing decisions every single day. I need some guidelines so I do not suffer paralysis by analysis.

It was with this in mind and with the experience of my YBN overall that I developed the following set of rules for acquisition of items from head to toe. These are my rules from now on. They might be useful for you, too. The method involves stripping down your current wardrobe and then sorting out needs from wants. This was thrust upon me by circumstance, but the lessons served me well. When you have pared back, simply carry on from there with this mantra playing always in the background: "Use it up, wear it out, make it do, or do without."

■ Achieving a healthy closet

Your goal is to truly know your wardrobe and to genuinely like what you see when you open that closet door. Ideally you will reduce your ownership to those items you like so much and that suit you so well that you will *want* to wear them again and again. Inevitably you will need less and you will wear what you have more often. Think of these as signature pieces that will give you an individual look that is totally "you," a defining presentation of self that makes you feel great. The end result is better for your wallet and more prudent stewardship of planet earth. Ready? Here we go:

- Get to know what's in your closet. Do not add anything until you complete this inventory.
- Throw a sheet on your bed and pull everything off the hanger. Immediately jettison those things that don't fit or should not have been bought in the first place, at least, not by you!
- Sort by type: i.e., blouses, pants, etc. Then sub-sort by colour. Pick the best of duplicate items. You might justify owning two crisp white shirts, but three? Why? Question each piece.
- Think carefully about what goes with what, using the rules from fashion magazines of a less profligate era. If those slacks don't pair up with at least three tops, they are not working hard enough for that place on your hanger. If a blouse cannot be dressed up or down, doesn't work in more than one season or under at least two jackets or sweaters, question its usefulness.
- Repeat the "setting out and getting reacquainted" process with shoes, the sweaters and T-shirts in your dresser drawers, your PJs, the coats in the front hall cupboard, and those "someday" clothes you have tucked away: cowboy boots, the leathers from your motorcycling phase, bridesmaid's dresses.

Really look at them and put the things you enjoy and that fit and suit you in an accessible place for stage two of achieving your ideal closet.

■ Scrutinize every item that remains; ironing, mending, repairing, or cleaning until you feel like it is ready to wear.

■ Now donate or give away everything that is not truly likely to be worn *within the year*. (See below for the exceptions; I do cut you some slack.)

■ Closet "keepers"

The exercise above requires discipline, but a well-edited closet is worth it. And there are exceptions to the rules above. Indeed, you should hang on to *some* things to help your basics work hard. Do not reject scarves of any kind on the basis of current fashion, especially if they are silk. Scarves take up little room so you can afford to wait for them to come around again. And they will. In the1960s, I owned a genuine Emilio Pucci scarf that I gave away as not "with it" in 1975. I really regret that decision now, as those patterns have returned to vogue *twice* since then, at prices well beyond the means of this budget-minded woman!

The second thing to hang on to is jewellery, on the grounds that it also works hard for the space it takes up and can make a look. Sometimes an individual piece is important enough to become your signature piece. Rona Maynard, the editor of *Chatelaine* for many of its best years, wore a pair of gnarly silver earrings every day. They were the perfect accent piece with her distinctive short-cut hair, and remain in my memory to this day. And while we are on the subject, keep an eye on what is being shown on the pages of the fashion magazines as a guide to what to keep out and what to tuck away for now. Costume jewellery looks are as fickle as fashion itself, ranging from chunky "gold" chains and jellybean bangles to delicate Victorian-retro pieces. Put yours away for tomorrow or you will wish you had.

Real jewellery (gold and precious stones) can be kept using the same rules as costume. Or if you need the money (and who doesn't?), sell when the price for a particular metal or gemstone is high. And don't think that only genuine gold, platinum, and diamonds should be your goal. In 2004, when she was already a Hollywood icon, Julia Roberts wore a striking brooch to anchor the sash of the Giorgi Armani gown she wore to the Academy Awards. She had the *fashionistas* abuzz over whose diamonds she was sporting. It turned out to be "just a little costume pin" she had tucked away in her jewellery drawer.

Finally, I admit there are some things that fall out of the realm of clothing and into family heritage pieces. We own an antique cream silk shawl that was used to enfold my father at his baptism, and that accompanied me down the aisle when I was married. If you cherish something of the kind, don't get crazy with family history.

■ Your own mini YBN – for clothing

Done? Now for the truly hard part. Simulate my YBN circumstances *for two months,* pledging to buy *nothing* and wear only what is on hand. This is your chance to get really intimate with what you own.

■ Plot your next day's "look" the night before. Think through accessories and jewellery, too. Put it all together on a hangar before you go to bed. You will find new pairings.

■ Keep records of how often you wore each item.

■ Make careful note of what is missing. For example, if those pants that make your butt look great were only worn once because, despite closet-bulk, you did not have a top that worked with them, a top would go on the list of possible acquisitions.

■ Make any list of purchases very specific. Don't just say "top for black slacks." Say "black-and-white floral top for black slacks, can go a) under dress blazer with skirt or slacks in winter b) pair with black or white shorts for summer and c) be worn with khakis in fall." Yes, I know this seems like an enormous amount of work to put into "a cute top," but you are building a better world by buying one top, not six, so deal with it.

■ At the end of the two months, review your list, but *do not* buy anything until you have truly identified your needs.

You may find you are already prepared to donate more items that didn't pass the test of "wearabilty." But do respect the seasonality of some things that may find their way back into your heart and onto your back when you have acquired the right pairings; a basic cream cardigan or black V-neck will do wonders for T-shirts and button-downs.

You are now ready to go out and acquire according to your own budgetary constraints and the ethical standards you have set in place. I am not going to set hard-and-fast rules for this portion of the exercise. But I will take you step-by-step through my recent experience, including the shameful bits.

■ What came after my year of buying nothing

Throughout my YBN, I kept a list of what I was going to acquire when unleashed on the retail world in January. Being a planner, I knew in advance exactly what I was going to spend. My objective was to spend half of what I might have spent in my YBN had I been buying. After all, it wouldn't have made a lot of sense to make up for lost time by splurging and doubling my purchases the next year. And I had learned a bit along the way about how and where I wanted to spend my money.

The average North American appears to outlay approximately $1,550 per person per annum on clothing and shoes. That is a statistical rough cut given that records are collected only by household and there are many variables at play. Women's spending exceeds that of men, by a third to a half, according to retail records, or approximately $2,000 a year for adult women. Household composition varies dramatically by demographics. The impact of a tiny baby on the family clothing allowance is, well, *tiny* (diapers falling elsewhere in the tally). The impact of a growing teen can be massive. Think of the price of name-brand sneakers!

On my list of clothing-related must-buys were some pretty

dull items like cotton (not slippery *polyester*) shoelaces for my walking shoes, and new basic underwear. But not all my buying was low-ticket. My job at the church and in the public eye continued, and I had wardrobe replenishing to do. I managed without a dress coat until I had done my homework. I found a good deal in January sales, a navy-blue wool brand-name coat. It was half-price and still cost more than one-third of my total clothing budget for the year. It is, however, a classic design, lined and warm. It should "do" for about eight years, if history is anything to go by.

Then I had great luck and found a pair of gently used non-leather black flats from a usually-too-pricey-for-me label. They look stylishly dignified peeping out from under clerical robes.

Those black dress pants had earned their rest. I donated them, replaced them, and added three more pair, bringing my dress pants wardrobe to five: one each of black, grey, chocolate brown, navy, and black-and-white "tweed." I got six tops in total to add to the 15 that survived the year. Each one was a strategic purchase and balanced out the wardrobe overall. I bought a soft grey "cashmere" sweater from the rack at the grocery store (perhaps not real cashmere?). A great find was an asymmetrically hemmed oatmeal wool tunic. Previously worn, it needed some invisible mending at which I am modestly talented. That and two new scarves to add to my collection will tie all outfits together.

My sources were assorted. Some came new from local small retailers, some second-hand from my favourite thrift place down the street, and some on a splurge trip with our daughter who has a far better eye than I do and is not afraid to shake her head if the item is not working for her mom. The total bill was $863. I may end up spending another $150 this year on sneakers and T-shirts, but my goal is to stick to $1,000, with less next year since there should be no big-ticket purchase (like the coat). I am happy overall and don't feel guilty. I am really enjoying what I own now and can think of dozens of different ways to wear the items.

A quick word about enlightened retailers. I made two discoveries and have undoubtedly overlooked many others.

First, Mountain Equipment Co-op is fastidious about their goods. My daughter had an MEC down jacket that had developed a zipper issue after three years of wear. She took it into the store to see if they could recommend a replacement zipper. They immediately swept that jacket off the counter and into their back room, replaced that zipper and had it back to her within the hour. For free. With apologies for it causing a problem in the first place. Impressive!

Second, while in England, I discovered Marks and Spencer had an imaginative policy with regard to trade-ins. If you bring them your old raincoat, for example, they will ensure it goes to a responsible recycler and give you £5 ($10 or more) toward a new one purchased from them. This applies to many pieces of apparel; check online for details. And watch for more innovative ideas. I suspect that there will be many more responsible retailers joining these two.

I do have regrets about one thing. I was *not* successful at finding things made locally or even on our own continent. Guatemala, China, Indonesia, Jamaica, and India vastly outnumber anything Canadian or American as a source for clothing. When I *do* find something that is made in our area, it is more likely to be a trendy design with a trendy little size to match. The exception is hand-crafted sweaters, fashioned by local artisans who make interesting things for "traditionally built" women and men. I urge you to keep an eye out for this sort of item and spend what you need to when you find an item you love. You will wear it forever. I have two such gems in my wardrobe. One of my two fall-spring outerwear items (the other is waterproof) is a locally made, handwoven, hooded thigh-length toggle-tie jacket. It is a cross between lemon and lime in colour and draws comments every time I wear it. I am proud to point folks to the tiny store owned by the woman who wove it. I saw author Margaret Atwood buying multiple items there, so I am not alone in my taste for the nubby look of textured yarn.

The other iconic handcrafted one-off I proudly wear is a Kaffe Fasset cabled mohair sweater-tunic in turquoise, seafoam, and violet. My husband gave it to me for my birthday 20 years ago. It still garners favourable comments. I am very excited that a new generation of knitters, both male and female, are creating wonderful garments that will still be a delight decades hence. The reintroduction of the yarn shop is one of the most heartening trends of the new millennium.

But it doesn't help when you are looking for jeans, or dress slacks, or that much vaunted cute top. It is frustrating. I would pay a premium to know I was buying something that gave jobs to local designers and manufacturers, as well as to retailers. I am not alone. Sadly, the days of the rag-trade industry in our own nation seem to be disappearing as international low-cost suppliers beat "Made in North America" on price every time. And we *do* buy based on the price tag these days. We all love a bargain. That is, on finished goods.

With that in mind, I toyed briefly with the idea of *making* that iconic cute top, as an alternative that might keep jobs in North America. But there is no relief in trying that tactic. The textile industry in Canada dropped from 50,000 jobs to fewer than 20,000 from 2004 to 2012. A quick scan of headlines on the U.S. industry, largely cotton-based, turns up phrases like "an industry in crisis." So even if I did buy a sewing machine (made in China), when I go to purchase my cloth, I would be buying from overseas suppliers and from factories that may well use sweatshop practices, as this is the industry most likely to utilize the very cheapest of labour.

I could stop buying altogether and simply cling to the clothing I have and wear itout until the threads fell off my body. If I said that was my plan, you might be fascinated in a horrified kind of way, but it is highly unlikely I could convert you to nudity. Being an ethical steward of what covers your own frame means making compromises. But they must be thought through. Your closet should not be a repository for your worst consumer impulses.

I will not replenish my wardrobe by buying new at the cost of the dwindling resources of our planet. I will not purchase with the same casualness I once did. My pledge is that I will try very hard to shop only according to the insights I have gained. I swear that I will stop and think *every single time* I buy something to put on my body or those of the people I love. Do I really need this? Is this item going to work for me this time next year? Is there a better fabric choice? Is there an alternative source for this item that is kinder to the planet?

■ Duty of care for your duds

My job now is to care for my clothes so that they *do* last, and so does the earth. To that end, I will close this section with another list, one that may guide you to better preservation of your clothing collection.

- Cold water is good for clothes, your budget, and for the planet. Reserve hot water use for things that are truly heavily stained, like gardening clothes or the things your kids play soccer in. Even then, try cold water wash first. You may be surprised. It is the agitation of your washer that really does the cleaning, not the water temperature and chemicals.

- Eco-friendly detergents are gentler for your laundry and the environment. And if you live on a septic system, you'd be insane to use anything harsher.

- Hang everything out on the line that you possibly can. What the heat of the dryer does to cloth is criminal, whether it be natural fabric or man-made. Line-drying is also healthy for your utility bill. It's good exercise and you will feel so in touch with nature. In winter, don't wimp out but invest in a wooden rack for indoor use.

- Think twice about dry cleaning *anything*. Once upon a time, I believed those labels they so cavalierly stick on wool, linen, and silk. I once routinely dry cleaned garments. I have since learned that my husband's and my own *unlined* wool slacks can be washed on a gentle cycle in cold water, hung to dry, and ironed back to nearly-new. This applies to unlined skirts, down coats (tumble dry on no heat), and many other items that sport the words "Dry Clean Only." Check a good online source for specific instructions.

■ Wash lingerie, silks, and woolens by hand, using pure soap (see "Part 3: Mineral" section). Hang to dry, or reshape sweaters laid out on big towels.

■ If you don't already know, ask somebody to teach you basic mending: button replacement, mending a tear, taking up a hem, even invisible mending.

■ Don't simply discard an item that gets marked with mustard or other yuck. Check out online sources for stain-removal techniques; think about clever camouflage with sweaters or scarves.

■ Take care of your shoes and boots by immediately wiping off road salt and spills, polishing and resoling when necessary.

■ When something fabric you love is tired, think about reformatting it into a quilt, cushion cover, handbag, or even just a patch to make something else more fun and interesting.

■ When a garment is terminal and not recyclable or donate-worthy, it's time to grow your ragbag. Don't chuck your garments in the garbage, to swell the landfill, unless there is truly *no* alternative.

And that's it for the animal side of your nature as expressed by your wardrobe. Care to join me in my YBN bathroom?

■ Chapter 2

Cosmetics, Toiletries, and Fragrances

THE SECOND TIME I EVER WORE LIPSTICK WAS TO ADD POLISH
TO MY GRADE EIGHT GRADUATION LOOK. As it was the first time
anyone had ever suggested I might be entitled to "a look," it was
a revelatory moment for me. The dress was purchased from a
smashingly "hip" big-city store that featured "mod" fashions for
conservative young people. A contradiction in terms you may
think, but hey, that's what the '60s were all about. It was the era
of mixed messages. Yes to "free love." Oh, and the rightness of
being, in your late teens or early 20s, someone's "old lady."
Hmmm.

The dress was a drop-waist, pink-and-white polka-dot piece
of dolly-bird heaven. My maternal grandmother went with me
to help select and pay for it as my graduation gift. She was a
talented seamstress and dress designer and, at 70, still followed
style with a passion belying a personality that seemed all Aber-
donian-Presbyterian-chill. On her night table one found, very
properly, a King James Version of the Bible and back issues of
The People's Friend, a Scottish publication best known for ser-
mons on morality thinly disguised as short stories and daily
prayers. Lurking underneath? *Vogue* magazine.

Though she was not a cozy grandma, she had her own style
and she had fostered that idea in my mother and aunt. She was
delighted that I knew what I wanted. She came as close to enthusiasm as I ever witnessed when I accessorized my dress with
lacy white stockings and pointy Mary Janes. Then, I was encouraged to purchase my first lipstick, from the cosmetic counter at the Rexall Drug Store on the corner. It was a very pale
shade of pink, precisely what Mary Quant (a top London fash-

ion designer) would have recommended. I liked it because it was exactly as seen in the much-thumbed copies of *Seventeen Magazine* Susan Forsey and I filched from beside her older sister's bed. Mum and Nana approved the purchase because it was modest and subtle.

My father, however, took one look at his first-born at the livingroom dress rehearsal that evening and shook his head. Not for the conventional reasons that daddies usually have – little-girl-growing-up, or "Oh, oh. Boys will be coming round soon." Nope. My father was and is, at 93, a connoisseur of pretty women. He looked at his just-turned-teen daughter and saw me as I would become. I had very dark, almost black, straight hair, cut in a bob. I had (and have) extremely fair skin. He went out on his own and bought a pure red lipstick and told me to try that instead of the *Twiggy* pallor. Even to my inexperienced eye, I could see the difference a clear cherry shade made to my face. And it suited "the look," too.

There are no photos of that much-vaunted event and an absolute river of cosmetics has run under my life since that long-ago time. But one thing never changed; my face demands a more assertive shade on the mouth. That's my look.

You probably know what looks best on you. If you don't, there are a dozen ways to find out. They all involve actual experimentation. You can start with what is being shown in the magazines or online, but you won't know whether that works for you without trying it. And I like trying things. For me, cosmetics are playthings for grown-up women. They are great fun and I love to have fun.

(I *could* have started this chapter by telling you about the *first* time I tried lipstick. I was three, naughtily experimenting with the pretty crimson tube at Mum's dressing table, smearing it all over my mouth. Mum walked in and nearly fainted seeing her beloved child apparently bleeding heavily. But I think we will agree, that's not fun!)

All this is to admit that I started my YBN far ahead of the game in this category. As it turned out, I had been hoarding eye makeup, glosses, blushers, and eye- and lipliners *forever*. I am a decades-long addict of these pretties and the drawers in our bathroom revealed as much. Some of you may remember the World of Beauty Club. I believe I must have been a charter member. A box would arrive in the mail once a month, chock full of interesting new items. They may even have been geared to one's colour, skin tone, and condition. Then again, maybe not. These refinements are more modern. I couldn't swear to it, but the drawers in my bathroom may have contained a few things leftover even from that bygone era. That box offered up a mashup of international brands, lesser-known domestic ones, and one marquee name-brand item each month – a real treat to an inveterate experimenter of "the look." A character in Jamie Mason's *Monday's Lie* admits to clinging stubbornly to the hot oil hair treatment she doubts she will ever use for any other reason "than that she'd paid good money for it." I get that.

I am not claiming that my stash contained much product dating back to the 1970s, the heyday of the World of Beauty Club, but there were some interesting finds in there. About half the items lurking in my bathroom cubby had never been opened. Few were actually so old as to have become toxic (more about intended toxicity later), but several smelled "off." I gave them the funeral they so richly deserved, though this turned out to be more difficult than I had counted on.

When I got down to doing the inventory that preceded each category entry point to my YBN, I began to feel sheepish. Why on earth had I ever collected five brow pencils, seven mascaras, 12 eyeliners, and countless shades of eyeshadow? I had only two shades of makeup and four blushers, as I had long ago settled on my regimen in that area, but the count on lipsticks, liners, and glosses was ridiculous: more than 50! A quick calculation suggested I had more than $2,000 worth of junk for my face alone shuffling round in those drawers.

If you asked me point-blank I would say I am not a vain woman. I am certainly no beauty, nor do I think myself any kind of fashion icon. I'm just a normal healthy person who likes to put her best face forward. I have known fashion editors who were known for and by their signature looks. I disappear in any crowd that includes the truly glamourous, which is fine by me. I don't have anything to prove and the first (and second) blushes of youth have long since passed. There is no justification for the amount I had accumulated; it gave me a shock.

When I revealed to friends and family that I was attempting my YBN, one pal mistakenly believed I was planning to go bare-faced for the entire time. "What, go without makeup for a whole year? Wow, are you brave!!!" she emailed me, disbelief in every exclamation point.

Well, no, I was not going face-naked. I had never contemplated that. The idea was that I would use up what I had and not buy anything new. Hey, not a problem with that horde! I set the record straight on my blog. But I was more thoughtful as I moved on to toiletries.

In my case, toiletries comprised a limited list of skin-care products, mainly cleanser and moisturizers. I had pantry-loaded the previous fall, when a local pharmacy ran a special on my favourite facial cleanser, reducing it from $7.99 to $5.50. I found I had half a large plastic tube, plus two unopened ones in January. I had only just switched a couple of years earlier from soap-and-water for my morning and bedtime facial cleansing ritual.

I do believe in keeping skin care simple. Confusing one's skin is the biggest cause of skin problems in my experience. My mother, of the near perfect complexion, lived her entire life with only a simple jar of Noxzema by her bathroom sink. She used it for makeup removal and as a moisturizer. She also slathered it all over my sister and me when we got sunburns, as children routinely did in that bygone era. I am convinced that it was not so much what was in the blue glass jars (eucalyptus, soybean, and linseed oil) as the simplicity of her routine. She didn't mess with her skin and, in turn, it left her in peace and looking terrific.

But bar soap and water made my skin feel too dry as I aged,

so I had switched to a mild cleanser-and-water routine that achieved the same level of clean, but that did not feel arid. I follow up with a drugstore brand daytime moisturizer (with added SPF year round), made by the same mass marketers as the cleanser. Despite the brand name, which has aspirations to clinical cleanliness, this manufacturer does not tout its bona fides as a "natural" cosmetic. Until recently, I had not been very aware of the great debate that lurks on cosmetic labels. I am sadder, but only somewhat wiser now. This is a minefield of new nomenclature that we will be visiting together in future paragraphs.

At night, I use a French-made night cream and eye cream. They are my indulgences, being both pricey and requiring a trip to the city, unless I want to add shipping charges to my bill, as this purveyor, along with everyone else, now markets online. I justify the expense with the pleasure I get from this jar – the packaging is sophisticated, the cream goes on silkily with little drag on the skin, and the fragrance is distinct but light.

Hmmm, I thought, that leaves hair products, knowing I had no shortage of these. We had rented out our home by the sea on a weekly basis as an income property until quite recently. As landlords, we learned some fascinating tidbits about the leave-behind habits of vacationers. One insight was that people leave three things when they depart: phone chargers, shampoos, and condiments. Afterwards, it is only the chargers they ever want back. You get to keep 19 different kinds of salsa and enough shampoo to open your own beauty supply emporium!

So I had plenty of suds, though I was low on the special one that keeps my all-white tresses snowy. That proved a challenge. It also provided me with one of the loveliest acts of kindness I encountered during the year. By November, I had completely run out of the blue shampoo essential to keeping white hair from yellowing in chlorine-filled pools. I am a swimmer. On one of the four visits that I had allowed myself to the wonderful Carol Nicol, haircutter to the stars (of Mahone Bay, Nova Scotia), she spotted the lacklustre situation of my locks. Knowing and being supportive of my YBN, she gifted me with a bottle of her salon blue-shampoo. Bless her generous heart!

Returning to the hair inventory, we come to conditioners. No issue. After that, I require no other product beyond a mousse for adding volume to my hair during blow-drying. That container seemed fairly full. So "no worries in the tub," I said, completely forgetting about bubble bath. And I am an advocate of the healing powers of the hot sudsy tub, once a week. (More often is cruel to your skin and the environment, and not too great for your wallet either!)

Both hubby and I are blessed with robust health and currently take no prescription medications. We had a good supply of aspirin, digestion aids, basic vitamins, cold remedies, and enough of the muscle relaxant we keep on hand for gardening and snow-shovelling aches. All okay there. Oh, and we had toothpaste, though I could have done with an extra brush; mine looked pretty wasted at the end of six months. Luckily, hubby had a scheduled cleaning at the dentist's and when offered his free brush, dental floss, and fancy-pants sample toothpaste, scooped them up with enthusiasm! And thanks to those travel minis, I had hand and body lotion galore.

In the rules for my YBN, I had stipulated that prescription medications would be allowed. I had previously endured two bouts of Lyme disease, both mercifully nipped in the bud by the right dose of antibiotics. I am one of the lucky ones for whom this was a totally effective remedy. But I had no compunction. If nabbed again with that telltale bull's-eye rash, I'd be making a quick trip to my Lyme-knowledgeable physician and getting a prescription. And we would keep our fingers crossed about any other emergencies.

As far as fragrance is concerned, I am very cautious these days. I had two small bottles of perfume to start the year and they are pretty much at the same level today as they were then. There was a time when I enjoyed fragrance a great deal. I "layered," as was advocated in the pages of the magazines: body lotion, deodorant, and perfume all from the same line. There was a day when I wafted a cloud of my signature scent. I sprayed and walked through it as I exited the bathroom to head out for work each day. I got compliments on my fragrance. But I had an epiphany in a theatre one night in the '80s. There was at the time (and still is) a perfume by Dior called *Poison*. It was wildly popular then, not everybody's cup of hemlock though, but heavily promoted and for a while, ubiquitous, the perfect combination to inspire those smell-alike knock-offs. The original was okay, just not my thing. The reek of the imitation that came off in waves from the woman seated next to me as I watched a Noel Coward revival that night had me hiding my face in my purse. It was truly nauseating.

I have wondered ever since if that was the effect I might have had on an innocent seatmate on some other evening? I hope my affair with fragrance didn't poison anyone. No one ever complained, but then, people didn't back then. They should have! I have no idea how many of the breathing difficulties attributed to scent are really caused by those products. But I dutifully respect the fragrance-free areas of our town and of my life these days. I save my perfumed moments for nights at home, where my husband's only reaction to my signature scent is positive.

Turning to the other things lurking in bathroom cupboards, I noted two things. First, I was not going to make any heroic attempt to go without toilet paper, or to come up with clever substitutes. We are on a septic tank, septic field arrangement and we have already learned to respect our environment. As my one disposable paper indulgence, I would continue to stock enviro-friendly TP.

On the other hand, we were down to three of facial tissues. And my husband and I mutually accepted that we weren't going to buy more. Break out the hankies! I had a good collection of cotton ones and so did my husband. No one is going to tell me it is more hygienic to use paper tissues than real hankies. Have you seen the bottom of some of those $1,800 handbags? Plus, if you define hygiene on a global basis, cloth wins (clean) hands down. Cloth handkerchiefs wash easily, though they are one of the very few things that I think *do* demand a hot-water cycle. My motto: have scads of hankies on hand and always use a clean one. (Confession: when our then-two-year-old grandson developed a cold in the winter of my YBN, I caved and got my husband to bring home the box of tissues he kept on his desk at work. Cotton hankies are no friend to the nose of a feverish two-year-old. There is an exception to every rule.)

I thought I had done a good job of listing the strengths of my inventory, but I had missed entirely some important items that became an issue later. Hand soap was okay. I had a half-dozen of those hotel-sized minis and some very fancy bar soaps that had been scenting my lingerie drawer. I used liquid soaps to refill hand pumps in the guest bathroom and at the kitchen sink. Not, I hasten to add, the anti-bacterial kinds, as the last thing our poor bodies need is more sanitization. We are in grave danger of killing off the very bacteria that keep us alive. Those pump containers do just as well when they are filled with diluted eco-friendly dish detergent, enhanced with lemon extract.

I had refills for my razor. I still wear a skirt from time to time and I think that after a lifetime of shaving my legs, I would continue to do so, even if they were not exposed. Silly, I know. But I long ago learned that disposable razors are the plastic devil incarnate, both financially and for the landfill. I buy my refills on sale and use them judiciously.

I had, however, forgotten to check my supply of multi-purpose contact-lens saline solution that gets used daily. And, as it was mid-winter and I was taking in as much sunlight as I could get, I omitted to predict the demand for SPF lotions that summer would bring. Finally, I messed up by not even thinking about bubble bath, thus creating, I shamefacedly admit, the lowest moment of the entire year. Challenges lay ahead.

■ Putting a good face on (for) my YBN

Clearly, I did not go without the goods to put on a happy face. If you have the patience for it, you can follow me on a detailed plan for how I made everything last the year through a strategy I call "cosmetic conservation." Here, then, is the daily routine I followed.

First the basics: cleansing, putting in lenses and applying moisturizer (well, I brushed my teeth, too). Towards the end of my YBN, I was getting so low on daytime moisturizer that I dampened my fingers with every application and poured out only a drop or two to make it last longer. Also, that cleanser in the squeezable plastic sleeve? When it ceased to flow easily, it turned out that a good third of the product was still hiding in the shoulders of that tube. I cut it in half, horizontally, scooped out my daily ration with a small plastic ice cream spoon, to keep things hygienic, and then squashed that top half back on again to ensure that what remained lasted that much longer. (The same trick works equally well for hand lotion that comes in the same sort of fat plastic tube.) I put this on the list of lessons learned.

Saline solution, or lack thereof, was a bigger issue. First, I looked up online how to make your own. If all you are doing is washing wounds or snorting it for the health of your sinuses, then feel free, go ahead and cook up a batch. However, even the keenest DIY websites shy away from recommending experimenting with their efforts for cleansing, storage, and hydration of contact lenses. Those that *do* tell you how to make your own solution suggest you make it fresh *every day*. And boil the bottles you keep it in daily as well. That just wasn't going to happen in my house!

Then I tried to tell myself that I could justify buying a bottle because it was only salt and water, after all, and therefore edible or, more accurately, potable. But since I wasn't going to drink it, that argument didn't hold (salt) water.

So I did the honourable thing. When I realized I had about a months' worth of solution and three months' worth of year left, I stopped wearing my lenses every day. My glasses work just fine. Though ancient (12 years old), they are neutral enough in appearance to "pass" and I can still see through them.

Back to the daily regimen.

My foundation was a drugstore brand that I blended myself

to get the completely correct shade for my particularly fair (okay, oddly pale!) complexion. Therefore, I always bought two at a time, decanted into a measuring cup to mix (with that otherwise useless tiny whisk from the kitchen set). I then poured the results back into the two little bottles. This may all sound dreadfully time-consuming, but since I only had to do it every couple of years, it wasn't that big a deal.

I never put makeup directly on my face. I always utilize one of those triangular sponges sold in bulk in cosmetic accessory aisles. Wash them with hand soap or shampoo first, or they will smell rubbery, and so will your face. Then, I dampen the wedges with a little tap water, scrunch up in a towel to dry slightly, and pour a drop or two of liquid foundation directly on the broadest part of the sponge. Then blend this on gently with the sponge, all over your face. The results should be so sheer that you are merely correcting for coverage, not truly colouring. I even use it over the spot where I will shortly redraw my eyebrows, now totally white in their natural state. They would otherwise disappear entirely.

If you are following along, you will find that you now have a bare canvas on which to create a masterpiece of cosmetic artistry. If you are keen, you can use a light corrector for under your eyes, and in the "marionette" lines created by smiling. I do this if I am going to be on display big-time, but not every day. Apply powder blush lightly, both on the apples of your cheeks and extending in a big curve up around toward your temple. Use a decent round fluffy brush, not that silly flat one that came with the compact.

Brushes in general are a good use of your money. If you have some, break them out on the bathroom vanity in a pretty container and you will use them more often, not just for special occasions. There are both synthetic and natural brushes available. Don't invest in a huge set if you are only going to use two or three. Usually for the price of less than a lipstick or two, you can get the ones you want. Washed regularly in mild shampoo, they last for at least two or three years, and much longer if you pay more. If you elect the pricier, natural-hair bristles, *do* look for a cruelty-free brand. This applies to any brush product. Increasingly, there are kinder alternatives with the same efficacy. A good set of brushes, well cared for, will extend the life of your cosmetics immeasurably and leave you looking more natural. Now you are ready for the fun stuff!

I had, as noted, lots of choice in the colour cosmetic spectrum. I did find that many of those seemingly endless tubes of lipstick (I did a cull first) were only half full. You will already have discovered the naughty trick that lipstick makers play on us, with vast amounts lurking below the surface. I think those product managers at Revlon, Maybelline, and Chanel are sitting there hoping that we will immediately run to the nearest cosmetic counter for a replacement the moment our lips touch the cold metal rim. There are ways around that. Fool them. Use a lipstick brush instead, and the other half of the good stuff you bought with your hard-earned dollars will be accessible to you.

Similarly, eyeshadow has a longer life if applied with a brush. But once it is actually on the eye, smudge it with your finger for a more natural look. I had no need to stretch my supply, but if I had had to do so, my trick would have been to use a good base under the shadow. These are slightly gloss creams, usually sold in small tubes that may or may not market themselves as eye-makeup "bases" or "primers." You simply squeeze the smallest amount on the tip of a finger and blend very, very sparingly from brow to lid. With a touch of colour for definition in the crease, you are good-to-go for the day. At night (or if your daily life includes something more glamourous than collating and stapling six copies of a church grant application), you can add a lighter shade on your lid.

Not being an everyday eyeliner user myself, I tend to stick to pencils as these are most likely to remain usable and not dry up. This becomes pertinent when, after a year, St. Patrick's Day rolls around again and you grab for the green one. The same applies to lipliners, indispensable as they are for keeping that brushed-on lipstick well-disciplined and not leaking all over any face over

50 years of age. The pencil style of all these items is cheaper to begin with, has less extraneous plastic packaging, and a quick turn in a sharpener will return them repeatedly to sanitized usefulness. Same with brow pencils: my favourite is probably ten years old despite nearly daily use. A light hand is what works best with all of these items. And, yes, you can pay $35 for a specially-marked "cosmetic" sharpener, but trust me, a regular pencil sharpener works just as well. Do keep it clean, though. Hydrogen peroxide is the thing to use for this purpose. More on this aspect of conservation in a later chapter.

Time for mascara. Again, I had no need to be stingy in my use of mascara as I had stored up quite a few. I have learned over the years that, for me (and, I suspect, anyone who is not an actress on daytime soaps) "washable" is kinder than "waterproof," when it comes to mascara removal. Once you are over 40, that sensitive eye area doesn't want to be scrubbed in a concerted effort to remove blackened residue. Any decent cleansing routine can and should remove the washable kind and that's all you want to be doing. Remembering my mother's rule, I figure the less fussing the less wear and tear. In my opinion, drugstore brands with the wand configuration you prefer are the best buy. I had a year to experiment with the seven I had on hand (including a couple of swanky testers from pricey lines). I kept returning to the same good old brownish-black washable in that familiar container.

And that was my beauty routine. By now you are either bored silly or have wandered off to try a new trick or two at the dressing table, so I am moving on to what I learned in just three more paragraphs. (By the way, for those who are keeping score, I solved the lack of sun protection problem by boldly asking my husband for SPF for my birthday, which luckily came in early July – rarely have I been so glad not to be a December baby!)

That bad moment induced by lack of bubble bath, you ask? There were extenuating circumstances. I was coming down with a cold and it had been a hard day that included meeting with a grieving family at church, sleet on the ground, and trying to support our (pregnant) daughter and her husband through a stressful renovation. It was late in the evening and I was really looking forward to that weekly hot tub followed by a soft pillow and a good book. I had one tablespoonful remaining of that very special bubble bath I order from England. This was the moment to treat myself. Unfortunately, one of the other things in the house that needed to be replaced but couldn't be because of my YBN strictures was a rubber bathtub disc, the kind that holds in the bath water in tubs without plugs. That once-pliable plug had lost its will to cling to the porcelain without careful attention until the water reached a certain level.

I put the plug in place. I turned on the water. I added my precious emerald green, horse-chestnut scented elixir of life. The phone rang and I answered it. Fatal! When I turned back, the rubber plug had run aground as the last of the hot water disappeared down the drain, taking the last few precious drops of my sudsy relief with it.

I swear, dear reader, I sat on the side of that tub and wept.

■ The issues we remove with tissues

So now that we have dealt with the ephemera, shall we speak of the less frivolous aspects of this need to put on a pretty face, this manifestation of the animal in all of us? What's it all about? Why do we ornament and anoint ourselves in this fashion? And what are the ethical, environmental, and health implications of doing so? You have more time in your life when you limit your shopping to the grocery store and don't hang out at malls, or bookstores, go antiquing, or indulge in window shopping. I learned a lot last year and I am putting my newfound knowledge to good use.

Both my daughter and her husband served, in successive years, as the presidents of the ecological society at the university they attended when they met. With another couple, and more keeners to come, they recently purchased a 50-acre farm that had fallen into neglect. They are resurrecting it, a few square feet at a time. After just a few months, the foursome already has both chickens and beef cattle. They are salvaging the apple trees that had long ago stopped fruiting. A full renovation of the century-old farmhouse has already taken place and there are garden plans aplenty. This is all in addition to the responsibilities of raising children, and full-time jobs outside the farm. My point is that these young people are dedicating their lives to salvaging what is left of our planet and making it productive again.

There are increasing numbers of such youth, and older ones too, who are committed to a lifestyle that is truly revolutionary. They are my heroes. They inspire me. There are books and online resources that will guide you to that more halcyon plane my young eco-pioneers will ultimately inhabit, if that is your aim. I am too old and set in my ways to make that leap. This, as you will already have recognized, is not a book that will take you to those places. It merely presents a way-station along the road.

My YBN nudged me up several notches from the ignorance in which I previously dwelt, to a greater degree of environmental and planetary respect. This section represents for me what was most revelatory of the vast divide between where we need to be going (i.e., where those young people are already headed) and where most of us are in terms of our consumer habits.

My beautiful daughter rarely sullies her face with cosmetics of any kind. She keeps lip balm of a blameless variety in her pocket in winter. She has lotion on her bedside table that is totally plant-based, made locally and with claims to be so toxin-free as to edible. She uses it on her hands and on her face as well, if she remembers. It smells like oregano. The family brush their teeth with a baking soda preparation. (My grandson once considered it a perk of a grandparent sleepover to get a swipe of our commercial toothpaste, but we have switched to a "clean" brand and give him two Smarties before brushing instead!) While she and I share the same values as to the importance of family, a belief in the necessity of being a compassionate citizen of the world, and have virtually identical approaches to food, I had never really understood her approach to personal care. To be honest, and to my everlasting mortification, I thought she was making a lot of fuss about nothing.

Turns out *I* was the one who was deluded. I will present evidence of how right she is and how wrong I was. In the previous chapter about clothing oneself, I dished out advice with a relatively clear conscience. After all, you *have* to cover yourself. But let's be clear. I *do* know there is no moral high ground when it comes to wearing makeup. No one *has* to wear makeup. I know that. Maybe someday, I won't wear it.

After listening to my argument for why you should let your face just hang out there, stark naked, you will have a choice to make. You can swear off makeup forever and, as our daughter's example suggests, lead a totally normal life.

Or you can search out brands that represent genuine alternatives and use them, and only them.

Or you can opt for a more earnest, earth-friendly, and self-protective edition of the "cosmetic conservation" strategy I introduced above. I have. I am stubborn, hedonistic, and getting set in my ways. But I am not foolhardy. My goal is to finish my existing stock and replace each item, if at all, with a "cleaner," less-harmful-to-me-and-this-planet version. And to use less of everything.

I don't know how much things will change in the personal care area for our generation, judging by my own stubbornness and those like me, combined with the intractability of the Big Boys – i.e., the largest manufacturers of beauty products. (And don't get on my case about gender stereotyping their executives as male. With embarrassingly few exceptions, they *are* male.)

We can, however, make a start and to that end I will attempt to point out some of the major problems with the personal care status quo, map out an interim compromise strategy, and then suggest ways you can access information about an alternative path for the future. I hope this might have appeal as a way to bridge the gap for a generation with usage patterns like mine, as revealed above. While I have elected not to pursue the highest goal of total abstinence, I am going to do better in this area for the sake of my own health and that of our planet. And I am going to drag as many of you with me as I possibly can. It was Jonathan Safran Foer who said, "If you take on a cause, you are spiritually obligated to advocate for it." Seems I am stuck with this one.

■ What's in that stuff anyway?

During my YBN, I set out to educate myself about where looking good ended, and being good began. After I came to grips with my profligate cosmetic acquisition habit, I made the decision to edit and downsize my collection of personal care products. I donated any unopened colour cosmetic and makeup items to a favourite charity: a group that assists women who are entering or re-entering the workforce. Unneeded soaps and the tiny shampoos, body lotions and conditioners from hotel bathrooms went to a homeless shelter. Those small containers are the best chance those without access to their own bathroom ever get to the daily feeling of being clean we take for granted.

And then I started trying to get rid of the excess unwanted product in a responsible fashion. This was the beginning of a revelation for me. First, I was going to do as I always had and rinse them down the sink. Luckily, some semblance of common sense stayed my hand, because I soon discovered that the responsible disposal of cosmetics is a challenge. The ingredients in beauty aids are as toxic as the contents of the pharmaceutical bottles they live beside in the family medicine cabinet. Here is what Lucy Siegle of the UK's *The Observer* newspaper has to say: "The best, yet imperfect, solution is to decant all unwanted toiletries into one jar and place in your normal rubbish. While there is evidence PPCPs leach from landfills, this is preferable to washing them away."

PPCPs? What were those? PPCP is the acronym for a growing cause of the pollution of our precious and increasingly endangered waterways. It stands for Pharmaceutical and Personal Care Products. Now, pharmaceutical pollution I knew about, and as a responsible citizen I took advantage of those times when local drug stores accept unused prescriptions and problematical OTC (over-the-counter) drugs for appropriate disposal. But the other things? Shampoos? Makeup? Facial cleansers?

"Hey, wait!" I hear you say. "I rinse those same things down the drain every day when I shower and every night when I wash them off my face." Yes, you do. And you, like me, voluntarily, happily, put them on your face (and likely eat some, too, along with your lipstick). Some sources claim we consume as much as five pounds a year of cosmetics.

This is where it started to get difficult for me to absorb the gravity of what I was dealing with. I had a hard think about what I and 95% of the women of my generation are doing to ourselves every single day. I looked in the mirror and said to myself, "You are putting chemicals and dyes *on* you that you would gag at putting *in* you." And somewhere from a distant biology classroom I recalled that skin is the largest organ of the body. And it is permeable. In fact, we apply lotions on our face each night *hoping,* indeed, *knowing* that they won't be sloughed off, but instead *counting* on the fact that they will be absorbed into the skin to keep us looking youthful.

The U.S. Environmental Protection Agency has much to say on the subject of PPCPs. Although illicit drugs, veterinary use, and agri-business contribute to the problem of pollution, what is the number one cause? The answer is human activity, as in bathing, shaving, and swimming. "The importance of individuals adding chemicals to the environment has been largely overlooked. The discovery of PPCPs in water and soil shows even simple activities like shaving, using lotion…affect the environment in which you live…People contribute PPCPs to the environment when … externally applied drugs and personal care products they use wash down the shower drain."

So much for leaving a light footprint on our beloved planet as I sluice off a day's worth of "pretty." At what cost am I achieving personal cleanliness?

Additionally, each one of those now-slightly-less-attractive-to-me products comes most frequently in a plastic container, cute as a button, but far less easily recycled as most also have metal parts. Mixed-material recycling is tricky stuff, trickier to manage than most consumer recyclers want to attempt. So it ends up in the landfill, leaching out the very toxins Ms. Siegle warned us about.

Then there is the issue of double- and triple-packaging. Think back to when you bought that new tube of lipstick. You had to haul it out, perhaps swearing, scissors in hand, from a cardstock-and-hard-shelled plastic package – mixed-material and unrecyclable. The harsh truth is that the manufacturers of cosmetics, toiletries and fragrances are among the least responsible when it comes to environmental protection.

Enough about the packaging, what about the contents? The ingredients of some of the bestselling brands of cosmetic confections are a list of unpronounceable poisons. You'd hesitate before exposing your Yorkshire terrier or Persian cat to p-phenylenediamine or sodium laureth sulfate. You'd ask the vet, "Is this really necessary?" before applying to that beloved pet. And you'd likely wear rubber or latex gloves, too.

Yet you shower daily with those chemical unpronounceables, or something like them. Every day you suds up your hair with them, sluice them over your face, rub them onto your husband's back at the beach, bubble bath your children in them, and gently powder them onto your newborn's tiny bottom. Unless you are way more savvy than I was, or live the sort of uber-aware, hypervigilant lifestyle of the more enlightened of my eco-warrior offspring, you may be totally unaware of the pretty poisons in your cosmetic aisles and your bathroom cupboard.

When I exited the women's magazine world back in the late '90s, there were early rumblings like thunder on the horizon, warnings of environmental problems for cosmetic, toiletry, and fragrance manufacturers. They were being hassled, as they saw it, by a somewhat looney fringe, who fancied themselves fragrance-sensitive and wanted to ban all scented products.

Groups that lobbied on behalf of the personal care industry were waging expensive communication campaigns to counteract these early warning signals, in what they feared might develop into a profit-threatening war. I helped them. With the research team of our publications, I developed a survey that revealed just how deeply evocative of positive familial memories perfume could be. This was and is simple psychology. You may recall fondly and like to buy things today that smell like the cologne you bought your dad every Christmas. You remember the scent your aunt sprayed on before a big date, impressing the heck out of a teenage you, and you will spend money to find that again. Perhaps you, like me, have buried your nose in the closet of a recently deceased loved one, just to spend another precious moment with that person. Yes, fragrance is a trigger of memory; that can't be denied. And a lot of wallets get opened as memories are tapped.

I also recall that my Nan's house smelled like shortbread. Surely I could bring her to mind by whipping up a batch of shortbread instead of sniffing some totally artificial, expensive, and deadly manufactured poison in an unrecyclable container? Would that I knew then what I know now. The words on these pages are the words I should have said to those Big Boys of the personal care kingdom, instead of dutifully toeing the party line as the boat headed for the falls.

Luckily, though good at my job, I wasn't good enough and the fragrance manufacturers lost that public relations battle. Today most hospitals, schools, and many workplaces ask people to refrain from wearing scented products, as a way to avoid triggering allergies. This was the progress made in the late '90s.

Since those early days, there has been significant work done in both education and the production of alternative products. Canadians are especially aware of the contribution of the David Suzuki Foundation and its characterization of the beauty industry as cavalier when it comes to health concerns. The report they produced on the toxins in cosmetics and toiletries in 2010 remains a landmark study. It is easy to find online and I urge those who are curious to read the backgrounders to the report. I have omitted much detail from the list below, which zeroes in on the "Dirty Dozen" – the 12 most dangerous ingredients contained in personal care preparations – but you can't help but notice the references to cancer, carcinogens, endocrine disrupters, and reproductive toxicant. I am not a chemist, to be sure, just someone who has sat at the bedside and held the hands of too many people dying from what may have been preventable disease. I have taken the following directly from the website.

1. BHA and BHT
   Used mainly in moisturizers and makeup as preservatives. Suspected endocrine disrupters and may cause cancer (BHA). Harmful to fish and other wildlife.

2. Coal tar dyes: p-phenylenediamine and colours listed as "CI" followed by a five digit number
   Look for p-phenylenediamine hair dyes and in other products' colours listed as "CI" followed by five digits. The U.S. colour name may also be listed (e.g. "FD&C Blue No. 1" or "Blue 1"). Potential to cause cancer and may be contaminated with heavy metals toxic to the brain. *In addition to coal tar dyes, natural and inorganic pigments used in cosmetics are also assigned Colour Index numbers (in the 75000 and 77000 series, respectively}.*

3. DEA-related ingredients
   Used in creamy and foaming products, such as moisturizers and shampoos. Can react to form nitrosamines, which may cause cancer. Harmful to fish and other wildlife. Look also for related chemicals MEA and TEA.

4. Dibutyl phthalate
   Used as a plasticizer in some nail care products. Suspected endocrine disrupter and reproductive toxicant. Harmful to fish and other wildlife.

5. Formaldehyde-releasing preservatives
   Look for DMDM hydantoin, diazolidinyl urea, imidazolidinyl urea, methenamine and quarternium-15. Used in a variety

of cosmetics. Slowly release small amounts of formaldehyde, which causes cancer.

6. Parabens

Used in a variety of cosmetics as preservatives. Suspected endocrine disrupters and may interfere with male reproductive functions.

7. Parfum (a.k.a. fragrance)

Any mixture of fragrance ingredients used in a variety of cosmetics – even in some products marketed as "unscented." Some fragrance ingredients can trigger allergies and asthma. Some linked to cancer and neurotoxicity. Some harmful to fish and other wildlife.

8. PEG compounds

Used in many cosmetic cream bases. Can be contaminated with 1,4-dioxane, which may cause cancer. Also for related chemical propylene glycol and other ingredients with the letters "eth" (e.g., polyethylene glycol).

9. Petrolatum

Used in some hair products for shine and as a moisture barrier in some lip balms, lip sticks and moisturizers. A petroleum product can be contaminated with polycyclic aromatic hydrocarbons, which may cause cancer.

10. Siloxanes

Look for ingredients ending in "-siloxane" or "-methicone." Used in a variety of cosmetics to soften, smooth and moisten. Suspected endocrine disrupter and reproductive toxicant (cyclotetrasiloxane). Harmful to fish and other wildlife.

11. Sodium laureth sulfate

Used in foaming cosmetics, such as shampoos, cleansers and bubble bath. Can be contaminated with 1,4-dioxane, which may cause cancer. Look also for related chemical sodium lauryl sulfate and other ingredients with the letters "eth" (e.g., sodium laureth sulfate).

12. Triclosan

Used in antibacterial cosmetics, such as toothpastes, cleansers and antiperspirants. Suspected endocrine disrupter and may contribute to antibiotic resistance in bacteria. Harmful to fish and other wildlife.

Scary stuff, right? But that was then and this is now, right? Everything will have changed now that *we*, the consumer, have shown *them*, the manufacturers, that we know what they are up to. The good folks who help you feel clean and beautiful will have immediately regretted the error of their ways and eradicated the listed toxins from their products. The cosmetic aisles of our city are safe to roam, debit card in hand, once again, aren't they?

The personal care business is a 60 billion dollar industry in North America. It is a very powerful contributor to the economic engine, supporting millions of jobs when you consider the retail (drug and department stores) and service industries (salons and spas) that also rely on these substances. Their lobbies to governments who make the laws that protect us are very powerful indeed. With few exceptions, these corporations are going to ignore us and defend and continue to do exactly what they have been doing until we, the customer, demand change with our wallets.

Frankly, though, many of us remain unconvinced and therefore we are not convincing. Knowledge regarding the toxins in our favourite brands is not shaking our confidence in their safety enough to keep us from buying them. The manufacturers claim that they test their brands and that they are safe if they are applied or used as directed. The FDA and Health Canada appear to concur.

Does this sound familiar? That a product can cumulatively have an injurious effect even when it is used exactly as it meant to be, that these same products are regulated and legal to sell... To me, this feels a lot like the time just prior to when the public realized that tobacco really *does* cause cancer. Smoking is injurious to your health. Smoking kills. What if cosmetic use is just as dangerous?

What is different is our complicity. We like the look, feel, and smell of "our" products and we don't want to be deprived of them. We don't truly believe they are injuring us, let alone killing us, because we all know someone who lived to be 102 and died with her lipstick on.

The personal care industry is not oblivious to the mixed feelings of their customers. They were well aware of a brief skittishness on our part a decade ago. Then they noticed our love affair with all things natural and they took great advantage of that. While researching this chapter, I lost count of how many people told me they were aware of the toxic ingredient "scare." Then they would reassure me that they now only buy products labelled "natural," "organic," "clean." Sorry, but you have been had. The beauty industry has taken full advantage of our fascination with natural ingredients. The cosmetic aisles blossom with images of greenery, references to herbal extracts, and the addition of organic ingredients. The words "clean" and "natural" appear repeatedly on labels. But they don't mean anything. Adding "organic rosemary oil" to the chemical cocktail that comprises your average shampoo is like sugaring strychnine; it's *still* poison. Unlike the legal strictures for the food industry, there is nothing that compels manufacturers to reveal the entire truth about what is in the bottles they sell.

Be wary. The corporations that provide personal care products are slipping things past us in a manner they would not be able to do if they were producing goods intended for consumption by mouth. Because of food-industry rules, when something is labelled "certified organic," for example, it means the product has met certain standards of agri-business definition, and perhaps even that the sites where it is grown, harvested, and packaged have been inspected. Nothing remotely like that applies to beauty products, which we also "consume" or "ingest" through our skin.

The beauty industry answers to only one thing: customer demand. As long as we continue to buy what they sell and ask for it to be shinier, sudsier, and to smell even more strongly of lemon-roses-sunshine-and-spring, they will continue to make it that way.

What *is* changing is the availability of knowledge about the potential risks. Better labelling by the personal care industry is being enforced, which means that if a product contains any of the Dirty Dozen most dangerous ingredients, those ingredients will be listed right on the product. There are other great sources of information too, for example, the book *No More Dirty Looks* by Siobhan O'Connor and Alexandra Spunt. Or check out GoodGuide.com for a truly easy-to-understand and useful list of both good and bad brands (though it lacks some of the Canadian entrants to the clean-beauty-product lineup). There are also Apps for your smart phone that will help you decipher personal care labels as you browse the aisles. I like one called Think Dirty (Shop Clean), which *does* feature Canadian items. By scanning the product code or by typing its name into the app's search engine, you can find out exactly how safe or tainted your list of personal care products is.

The reason I like all of these sources – the David Suzuki Foundation, O'Connor and Spunt's book, the GoodGuide, and the Think Dirty app – is because they don't require me to be a chemist to figure out what to avoid.

When it came to my own list of personal care products, I was appalled. Practically everything I have used and would have liked to continue using scored a "ten" for maximum toxicity, allergen potential, and all-round badness. To be fair, the Think Dirty algorithm holds to very high standards. Anything with the ingredient "fragrance" listed (usually at the end of the list) automatically rates as a worst offender. "Fragrance" in this context is a catchall term that allows the product's maker to conceal exactly what chemical additives go into the scent "package," often a combination of things that can be found on the Dirty Dozen list. I tend to check Think Dirty first and then see if that bad rating is earned entirely from the fragrance factor by double-checking with the GoodGuide app.

By the way you cannot avoid this hazard simply by seeking out the words "unscented" or "fragrance free" on labels. The presence of those words does not necessarily imply an absence of chemicals, often merely the addition of others designed to mask the scent of smelly ingredients. The issue of fragrance is definitely a complicating factor when trying to judge the lack of toxicity in your favourite product.

■ So much for Beauty: dealing with the Beast

I was an enabler of the schemes and strategies of the main-stream cosmetic industry for many years and now I am not (or at least, I am much less so). Although my time in the communi-cations industry had rubbed off some of my naivety when it came to the lengths that corporations will go to sell us stuff, I now see that I remained stubbornly skeptical of those who spoke about toxins in our toiletries for far too long. I admit I saw them as spoilsports who were trying to take away something from me that I had found to be a great pleasure. The time I spent trying on eyeshadow and experimenting with fragrance layering was time well spent in my book, a kind of personal creativity, with my body as palette. I was the willing victim of an industry that does not have my best interests at heart, yet.

I suspect that there is a lot of scrambling going on in the research labs of major personal care companies today, to be ready to market safer product lines. I am not the only one who will be voting with my wallet and boycotting products that offend toxic-ity rules. You can already see there is competition for the big drugstore and department store brands offered nationally by re-tailers such as Whole Foods. In our small city, Pete's Fruitique and Organic Earth are two stores that carry a wide range of beauty products, hair and facial care, and deodorant choices that do *not* carry the ingredients listed on that Dirty Dozen list. If you do not have access to these, check out a store that sells health foods. Or go online. There is a whole new range of prod-ucts (from A–Z) brought to you by these and other folks: Aubrey, Aura Cacia, Basicare, BWC (Beauty Without Cruelty), Burt's

Bees, Biotherm (a cross-over brand), Dr. Bronner, Dr. Hauschka, Gabriel, Green Beaver, Kiss My Face, Lip-Ink, Mario Badescu, Now, Sappho, Toms of Maine, Weleda, and ZuZu.

Admittedly some of the packaging, marketing, and promotional efforts of the new clean-and-safe personal-care kids on the block are not going to live up to the lavish efforts of the traditional big brands. Many lack the pizazz we associate with this industry and some appear old-fashioned or medicinal. But if you and I keep supporting them, they will get more creative and develop market savvy. I particularly commend Lip-Ink, Green Beaver, Kiss My Face, Mario Badescu and Weleda for making terrific progress in presenting their product lines with a sophistication lacking in earlier efforts from the fledgling cleaner-safer industry. Watch for additions to the offerings coming out of Europe. The EU has put in place standards that have spawned a host of innovative new products from that side of the world.

Neither should we discount the possibility of healthier alternative products emerging from the Big Boys, companies like Unilever, Johnson's, and P&G. If you seek long enough in the safer cosmetic online guides, you will already find the occasional appearance of players such as Avon, Maybelline, L'Oreal and The Body Shop. Some of these are deliberate. Johnson's worked very hard to come up with non-toxic baby bathing products after being slammed by the media on behalf of consumers shocked to discover they were slathering poisons on their little ones. Others are, I suspect, unintentionally present with product lines that almost incidentally do not contain the worst ingredients. Certainly, thus far there has been little effort out of the larger manufacturers to promote major brand extensions as "toxin-free." After all, what would that imply about the rest of what they market to us?

You may be wondering why I have not mentioned my favourite medium, magazines, as a source of the latest information about toxicity in standard beauty products and/or the introduction of innovative new ones. There is a good reason for that omission. By and large, major magazines aimed at women depend heavily on the cosmetic, toiletry, and fragrance industries for vital advertising dollars. They have publishers (I know because I was one) terrified of biting the hands that feed them those vital advertising revenues. The same is true of television. With the exception of NPR, PBS, and our own CBC, networks not solely dependent on ad dollars, there are few broadcasters brave enough to dish the dirt about unclean cosmetic products. And the new fledgling companies that *do* have product entries in the "clean" category lack the budget to challenge the Big Boys.

Why don't magazine executives encourage their beauty editors to speak about these things with the same frankness that food editors speak of the challenges posed by commercial products in the supermarket aisles? There are two factors at play. The first is that the grocery products we consume through our mouths are subject to far greater government and industry scrutiny than those we consume through our skins. The second is that the Big Boys of the beauty business currently offer vastly fewer alternative product lines than the food industry does.

For example, our daughter is celiac, but many people eat gluten-free by choice. Major magazines aimed at both men and women have spoken freely about gluten-free diets. The grocery product industry has responded by offering cake mixes, frozen dinners, flours, crackers and pastas, all proudly labelled gluten free. And these are *major* manufacturers like Robin Hood, Blue Diamond, President's Choice, and Duncan Hines. Those packaged-goods producers saw a consumer need and, sensibly, rushed to fill it with product. They, and others, have done the same with trans-fat free, lower sodium, and sugarless offerings of margarine, soups, soft drinks, and confectionary items – specialty goods to feed the needs of those requiring or preferring alternatives. And producers premium-price them so presumably even though quantities are far fewer than their standard lines, the profit margins are high enough to ensure an ongoing and growing supply.

Why, then, does the same thing not happen with shampoo, for example? *Because food manufacturers can supply an alterna-*

tive without implying that their mainline brand is toxic. And the food editors can speak supportively of the need for *some* of their readers to lower their salt intake and offer brand-name suggestions, without suggesting that the mainline brand is death-in-a-jar. It is both as simple and as dramatic as that.

So when you as a reader or viewer cannot count on your usual source of information for personal care products to enlighten you, where can you go? I have already named some useful sources above, but my hope is that there will be increasing discussions of the issues in the pages of the mainline magazines. I truly believe that there are good people working in the beauty industry and writing about these products, and that they have consciences and will not remain silent. (I told you I'm an optimist!)

In the meantime, and beyond the logical aspects of not applying to my face or body something I wouldn't want to touch with my bare hands (the "ick" factor), the support of toxin-free brands by those most serious about preventing breast cancer provides me with additional motivation to change my ways.

We all know someone who has died of breast or another form of cancer. Unless you are deeply incurious, you will have puzzled over why there seems to be so much cancer in the world today. While it is encouraging that there are more and more survivors as treatments improve, it is a slam-dunk that we'd all prefer not to get that diagnosis in the first place.

While I do not claim to know for certain that there is a direct link between the use of certain personal care products and the increased number of cancer diagnoses in our generation, I won't risk my health and that of my family. I gave up smoking many years ago and moderate my eating to avoid illness. Why on earth would I risk anything for one more shade of lip gloss or shinier hair?

Luckily, I don't have to and neither do you. There are several things we can do to mitigate the effect of the bad things in personal care products that make us look good.

■ Vow to go through your stash of personal care products and check them against one of the unbiased lists as described above. Get rid of (in the most environmentally-correct way, possible, please) everything that is truly a disaster: anti-bacterial anything, talcum powder, baby/children's products of any type not guaranteed to be safe by the Dirty Dozen rules.

■ Practise "cosmetic conservation." Use less of everything else.

■ Go without makeup when you don't absolutely need it.

■ Re-apply your lipstick less often. Use a "safe" lip balm between rounds.

■ Take fewer baths and showers. Your skin will thank you and so will the water table.

■ Use moisturizer only every second night and deodorant every second day.

■ One shampoo is enough unless you were at a smudging ceremony prior to your shower. Those words "rinse, repeat" were the single biggest contributor to increased profits for haircare products ever. And they are totally unnecessary.

■ Dilute (with water) shampoos, body washes, conditioners.

■ Don't buy specialty products. Your neck can't read the label and doesn't suspect it needs a sole-purpose cream.

■ Promise yourself that as a tube, jar, or bottle empties, you will either not replace it at all, or you will seek a better, cleaner alternative.

■ If you, like me, have enlightened children and they don't give your grandson bubble baths, or use anti-bacterial soaps, or permit commercial toothpaste in their homes, when they come for sleepovers *respect their wishes*. If your children don't hold these views, *discuss the issues with them*, gently, persuasively, gifting them with safer alternatives to the problem products they *do* use. And if your kids and grandkids ask why they are having a bath with *Dr. Bronner's Baby Mild Liquid Soap* rather than some other more colourful bubble bath, tell them it is because you love both them and this planet.

■ Strike traditional toiletries off the list of gifts you give. You don't need to be an enabler and you don't need to fill someone else's lungs with toxic talc, pretty soaps that are pretty poison in disguise, and scents that suffocate the sensitive.

■ Tell your children and grandchildren and the offspring of everyone you know, especially the girls, how beautiful they are *as they are*. Do this often and sincerely. They need to be prevented from thinking that they are only at their best when they are enhanced.

A new friend, a recent partner to an old high school pal, did me a great kindness during my YBN. Though we had met only twice before, we had bonded in that no-nonsense way women of a certain age have, knowing what we need from a friendship and immediately spotting the potential. She knew my penchant for whiling away my time at cosmetic counters and realized that this was something I would be studiously avoiding over the months of my YBN. She and her partner called when they came through town on business. My husband and I went out to lunch with them and laughed until our sides hurt. Towards the end of the meal, I noticed Christine pull out an attractive cosmetic bag from her capacious handbag. She presented it to me with a broad smile. I recognized the styling right away as a GWP (gift with purchase) from one of my favourite beauty-aid manufacturers. In it, she had assembled a fine collection of samples, pretty accessories, a full-size lipstick, and a tiny palette of fresh new eyeshadows. I treasured her thoughtfulness. When next I see Christine or any other of my friends (and I am blessed with some grand ones), I am going to assemble a similar bag and present it. Only mine will be chock full of the safer, cleaner product offerings available.

In the future, I plan to still enjoy the world of beauty (who needs a club?). But I will make my buying decisions based on concerns for recycling, sustainability of ingredients, and non-toxicity. The beauty of beauty products is far from just skin deep.

■ Chapter 3

Gift-Giving and Nest Making

■ Gifted giving and re-gifting

MANY ANIMALS OFFER GIFTS TO THEIR OWN KIND AND TO MEMBERS OF OTHER SPECIES WITHIN THE ANIMAL KINGDOM. This is Mother Nature at her most generous. For example, the male nursery web spider (*Pisaura mirabilis*), commonly found in European grass meadows, wraps offerings of seed husks in silk, scented with pheromones, both products of its own body, and offers these to a prospective mate. Now that's a way to get a girl's attention! And those of you who have earned the respect of a house cat (no small achievement) have probably been the lucky recipient of the odd mouse or bird carcass, ceremoniously proffered for your appreciation.

Humans, too, like to offer gifts and I am a very human animal. I cherish the hunt for the exact perfect item for those I love. I freely admit to being a ham-fisted wrapper so that's never been part of the thrill for me (perhaps I should try silk?), but I love that big reveal. Half the pleasure of gift-giving is seeing the recipient light up with pleasure. Often that pleasure is doubled; first, delight at receiving a fitting item and, second, gratification at being understood and treasured by the giver. "How did she know I would like a subscription to *F1* magazine!?" For that reason, I don't like to miss a family member's birthday and I try to take care to mark the occasion with a little something special. And then there is Christmas: a season that beyond its spiritual significance whets my appetite for matching the exact right thing to the exact right person.

Given this, my YBN seemed at first to have poured a giant bucket of cold water on a huge pleasure centre in my life. I had to sit down and have a serious think about how to jump this hurdle. And I didn't have long to mull it over, because my son-in-law's birthday is January 9.

The gift I ultimately came up with produced one of the high points of the year for me. A little background: my daughter is celiac and therefore they keep a gluten-free kitchen in their home. Earlier experiments in permitting other kitchen users to have access to items containing wheat resulted in a couple of disastrous cross-contamination incidents. Her husband and others in the household are now very respectful of this. But everybody longs for a good chomp on a piece of whole-wheat bread from time to time and I *do* love to make bread, both in my machine and by hand. I love to experiment with recipes, adding new ingredients to tried-and-true favourites, and switching things up. I release a lot of stress while kneading a lump of dough. I really enjoy the smell of bread baking. Who doesn't? And there is something quite close to heaven in eating that first, warm-from-the-oven slice. I treasure my bread machine, too, and will tell its story in a later chapter.

You can see the first gift was easy. I pledged that I would provide my son-in-law a loaf of fresh bread every Monday. He could take it to the kitchen at work and make it a staple in the lunch he made for himself daily anyway. Throughout the year, I added a label to each one, with suggestions of what sort of meats, cheese, or veggies went best with that particular loaf in my experience, and he would experiment and give feedback. As the year wore on, I learned that the Three Cheese Bread, the Seedy Spelt Loaf, and the Rosemary Rustic were his favourites.

I didn't know just how truly successful this gift was until the summer. I was invited to address a luncheon speaker's series that his office hosted once a month. The topic was, of course, my YBN. I walked into that room and was swamped by questions: "Are you the lady who makes the great bread?" "How do you get the rosemary flavour so pronounced?" (Use a mortar and pestle on whole rosemary, not ground, just prior to adding to the dough.) "Will you make bread for me if I bump Alex off and marry your daughter?" (Umm ... no.)

It was a gratifying experience, an emotional high I had been afraid would elude me during my YBN. I got into it, over the course of the year baking bread, cakes, and cookies as gifts for loved ones. I preserved the gifts of our newly revived crabapple tree: spiced crabapple jelly is amazing with turkey. Maple cream fudge and molasses candy were well-received Halloween goodies, for people I knew. (I did not try to give strangers who came to the door homemade candy!) The blackberries that my grandson and I picked in the fall made superb "cassis" to add to the Christmas Prosecco (Italian white sparkling wine).

Although not a skilled knitter like my mum, I turned out scarves with scrap wool I had on hand, trading and bartering with pals who knit from intricate patterns. Strictly amateur, I have never mastered reading a pattern, so I stick to afghans, neck-warmers, and headbands. They are the perfect way to use up leftover yarn.

I also did clever things (well, I thought they were clever) with needle and thread: affixing a crest from a much-loved but worn-out T-shirt to a toque, turning sheets into duvet covers, covering tired pillows with fabric and prized favourites from the button-box. I finished embroidery projects that dated back 15 years. Anything that came to mind that might fit into someone else's life left my hands happily. Over the year, I drained the supply of bits and bobs that had swelled my crafts cupboard for years. And it felt really great, as if I was communing with an earlier time when the gifts of one's own resources were the only gifts there were.

A modest skill with a paintbrush came in handy both for gifts of small watercolours, and for cards. My husband got a framed image of a heron that fishes off our dock as a Father's Day gift. The cards were well-received in the main, though my father's hand-painted card did not go down as I had hoped. I heard from my sister that my nonagenarian dad had not quite grasped my YBN philosophy. Upon receipt of his birthday card, he immediately phoned her, quite concerned that we were in such poor financial shape that I was resorting to handmade greetings.

The other way I satisfied the needs of a community of would-be recipients was through re-gifting. Now, this practice *does* require either excellent note-keeping skills, or a very good memory. I have neither skill, so if I accidentally gave you back something you earlier gave to me, please forgive me. There, now that that's out of the way, allow me to pass along a couple of helpful hints.

■ Keep your re-gifting circles separate from one another. If you fail to follow this rule, you could end up offering that unsuitable scarf that Mary gave you to Mary's own sister. You might offend both of them.

■ Please do not re-gift toiletries and fragrances that do not score well on the safe personal care items guides like GoodGuide, or Think Dirty/Shop Clean (see Chapter 2). Passing on a problem does not make it less of one and if you read this book, you can no longer pretend you don't know the difference. Discard unwanted toiletries using the appropriate rules for your area and the container.

■ It is always okay to re-gift gently used books. You can even say, especially to a very dear friend or young person, "I wanted you to have your own copy, because I loved this so much (when I was your age)." Unless you are very sure of the tastes of the recipient, don't put inscriptions in books because that just makes re-re-gifting awkward. And we *do* believe in the pass-along element of books, don't we? It's a crime to have them mildewing away somewhere instead of circulating. Check out the Little Free Library movement in your area; that's donating, not perhaps re-gifting as such, but the same idea.

■ When your own children give you something, no matter what their ages, think long and hard before re-gifting, unless you are certain you can keep it to yourself. I loathe truffle chocolates, but my daughter forgot and gave me some for my birthday. (Was she re-gifting? I hope so, because they were expensive!) I *did* give them to someone else, but when she asked me if I liked them, I felt compelled to "fess up." I could see she was taken aback, as she had genuinely forgotten my silly preference for milk chocolate over the good stuff. Should I have composted the darn things, and recycled the box, without her knowing? When I first met my future mother-in-law, I complimented her lima beans (which I do not like at all). I condemned myself to a lifetime of consuming Lima Bean Supreme at every family dinner. Being good *and* truthful is complicated.

■ Anything that is truly personal should not be re-gifted without notifying the giver. Your great-aunt's jewellery presented by your mother to you as a token of her own memories of her aunt should not be passed along to anybody else while your mother is still living. That could cause real damage to family relationships. After that generation passes away, however, unless there are complicating factors, sentiment can and should, in my humble opinion, be quashed in favour of utility. If you are truly never going to wear that chunk of gold shaped like ice skates beloved by Great-Aunt Jane in her lifetime, do not let it languish in the back of a drawer to be discarded as costume junk by the next wave of your family. Get it to a gold re-seller and use the proceeds to give the gift of skating lessons to a young person in Jane's memory.

■ Everything else is fair game and only people who own gift shops would dare to tell you re-gifting is tacky. It is much more evil to squirrel things away for another generation to find when you are gone and throw into the landfill completely untouched, unused and unloved.

If you have already used up your store of "re-giftables" and are not inclined to domestic crafts as a source of gifts to satisfy your needs, there remain a host of alternatives that allow you to participate personally in the gift-giving process. From gardeners, there is the gift of seeds or seedlings, produce or flowers from your own garden. From woodworkers, the gift of a shelf or a bird feeder would be welcomed by most recipients. From techies, an hour's tutorial to teach the recipient how to use a new program or device. (One work colleague showed me how to get the most out of Twitter and Facebook for promotional purposes and another taught me how to program my new VCR. Now *those* were gifts!)

How about the gift of good old-fashioned labour like weeding, raking, snow shovelling? Or services that the recipient would otherwise have to pay for; for example, the gift of a promissory note for babysitting, manicures, closet organizing? My dear friend Sarah hosts great parties, and is especially known for her knack with unique and delicious appetizers. She amasses a collection of fabulous condiments over the course of every year. To repay Sarah's hospitality, twice now, when her sister Jean has come to visit, we spent a happy couple of hours cleaning out Sarah's refrigerator for her: checking best-before dates, disposing of bygone brie and outdated pecorino, and then scrubbing down the whole thing ready for a new season of events. You can really bond when betting on how many flavours of mustard are hidden in that fridge this year. The point is to cut your gift coat to fit your talent cloth.

If you are pressed for time, by all means *do* consider gift cards or certificates. Think local businesses first: restaurants, cafés, and takeout places that are *not* chains need your trade and that of your recipient. I gave cards for local groceries at Christmas to family members during my YBN. It was a fundraiser for our church so everybody benefited. It was guilt-free for me as I wasn't encouraging acquisition of useless *stuff*. Everybody has to *eat*. One of the best gifts I received during my YBN was a gift card for a much-needed pedicure at a salon that avoids chemical sludge in their treatments, courtesy of my savvy child.

Certificates for haircuts, massages, and salon services seem defensible. I am loathe, however, to give gift cards for retailers offering only finished goods, as opposed to services, but you could make a case for some exceptions. Ecologically-minded and dedicated new parents of infants will require diapers. Cloth diapers are pricey, so a gift card for a local supplier might just keep a load of dirty plastic/paper out of the landfill.

To change the subject completely, people who like to give parties need to buy supplies. We have local vintners and distillers who would love to meet a new customer introduced via your gift. The thing is to think the act through before you buy something whose only good end might be to be re-gifted. Why add another layer to a drawer of useless *anything*?

■ Feathering your own nest

I used the same sort of approach to assuage my guilt over any nesting issues that came up during my YBN. I speak here of home décor, not the potential purchase of appliances or furniture, which I have categorized under "Mineral" (Part III).

Here is a list of some of the things I would have been tempted to buy had it not been my YBN, and how I got around these needs. Who am I kidding? Had temptation entered my mind, and had it not been my YBN, I would have lined up at the store and *waited* to pay! Buying things for my house always seemed downright altruistic to me, before my YBN. As Christopher Marlowe wrote, "But that was in another country: and besides, the wench is dead."

- Dishcloths wore out and looked quite dispiriting by the end of the year. I ignored the problem for a long while, eked out another while by bleaching them with hydrogen peroxide, and then gave up. Then I got inspired and used up a ball of cotton yarn to make new ones.

- When tea towels looked really tired, I transferred the oldies to the ragbag and got out the souvenir ones, with recipes, maps, and sayings on them that I had stashed away. *This* was that rainy day.

- Our bathroom towel sets are getting a bit long-in-the-thread. Some were crying out to retire as rags. Bath-, hand-, and wash-towels sets, however, do not all wear at the same rate, so I had to change the habit of a lifetime and break them out of their families. This was an emotional challenge. I recall vividly a time growing up when our family passed from being financially straitened to relative comfort. My mother marked that proud moment by purchasing a set of matched towels through Pinky Stamp Books, at the local Steinberg's Supermarket. I felt I had let down the side when I hung a mismatched group a mere generation later. (Note to others of my vintage: matchy-matchy is not the way that youth live. You might as well give up trying to gift them with sets.)

▪ Sheets. Ditto the above. When normal wear and tear set in during my YBN, I kept my best linens for guests and had fun mixing it up with family bedding. I practised the ancient and painstaking art of invisible – okay, sort of invisible – mending on bottom sheets to extend their lives. When they expired anyway, I sewed the orphaned top sheets together to make a duvet cover.

▪ Rather than buy flowers for the dinner table, which is a sin explored shortly, cut pussy willows in late winter, garden stuff in summer, and colourful foliage in the fall. My grandson and I had fun making twig, feather, and yarn dream catchers for the Thanksgiving table.

▪ When I ran out of "good" candles, I used a bag of tealight candles in ancient cups leftover from cup-and-saucer sets prized in former generations, and collecting dust in our basement. I used up a box of utilitarian "emergency" white candles by dressing them with a bit of ribbon stuck on with a hot glue gun. A cautionary note: blow candles out *before* they reach the ribbon.

When it comes to larger items to beautify your home, as opposed to simply tweaking an existing look, there is a whole world of books and wonderful websites on *upcycling*. Europeans are way ahead of North Americans when it comes to this practice, defined as "the process of converting waste materials or useless products into new materials or products of better quality, or for better environmental value" (Wikipedia). I commend their imagination and innovative techniques. More about this movement in "Minerals."

■ You don't bring me flowers anymore

And I wouldn't thank you if you did. Back to the issue of buying flowers. This was something I found out during my YBN. Maybe you read about it, too? I had a bouquet of cut flowers on my dining room table that had been the hostess gift of a dinner guest the night before. I was showing them to my young grandson and getting him to name the colours of the various shades of tulip, when I noticed my son-in-law hovering a bit and flinching. As he is always the very definition of courtesy, I quickly picked up on the fact that he didn't want the lad getting too near the flowers. I obligingly changed the subject and vowed to follow up. But it took me a while. Here is what I found out.

The growers of cut flowers are among the heaviest users of agricultural chemicals and this includes use of the most toxic of pesticides. More depressing still, those nursery centres that spring up everywhere when the snow melts? They are selling garden plants that are pre-treated with the very pesticides that could be most lethal to bees. Which we then obligingly bring home, thus passing on the problem to our local apiaries (beehives). Our bees are already troubled enough by neonicotinoids. They don't need another dose caused by my impulse buy of parking-lot impatiens on the way to the car.

Additionally, there is a growing body of scientific literature that suggests that many allergies to flowers and plants could actually be a reaction to the toxins in which the plants are soaked, rather than to the green things themselves. More disturbingly, journals as varied as the *International Journal of Environmental Health Research* and the *Journal of Environmental and Occupational Medicine* have published studies revealing illnesses symptomatic of pesticide poisoning in florists and in garden workers from the fields that produce those flowers and the plants for our gardens. Many of those seedling plants and those flowers for wedding bouquets come from such faraway places as Columbia, Ecuador, Ethiopia, and Kenya, thus adding to the negative impact on the clean air and earth of our planet.

These factors add up to a mighty high price to pay for a bunch of pretty buds!

Seriously. Don't bring me flowers anymore. For my part, I won't send them to my dear stepmother for her birthday; there is a lovely scarf I can knit that is even more colourful. I will grow my flowers if I really am so moved, and from organic sources. Not only will the bees and butterflies be happier (especially with my tomatillos and my milkweed), but that grandson of mine can handle any flower or plant that he wants in the garden or gracing my table without fear.

■ Toys-aren't-always-us

The keen-eyed among you will have noticed that most of my gift-giving has conveniently avoided the youngsters on your list. It is very hard, as parents, and perhaps even more difficult as grandparents, to resist the buying signals sent out along with the Letter to Santa, or to ignore the blandishments of the birthday party. How can you not give Brenna the Barbie-Thing she wants above all else? Why should Tim be the only little person in his circle not to have the full Thomas-the-Tank-Engine collection?

I have already ranted on this subject in the Introduction, so I will keep this short and practical. The care and protection of our children and grandchildren means avoiding that plastic-fantastic-brand trap. If we coat the earth in this junk, future generations won't be able to dig their way to soil and grow a single potato or leaf of kale. (And even if you, like me, think this latter loss is not such a bad thing, they should at least have the chance to try!)

We are already poisoning the oceans. I came across the following particularly-apt and sobering news item from *BBC Newsmagazine,* by Mario Cacciottolo (July, 2014). It describes a child finding a small flower on a beach in Cornwall, England, but not the kind we hope our children will discover and press in a book:

It is one of 353,264 plastic daisies dropped into the sea on 13 February 1997, when the container ship Tokio Express was hit by a wave described by its captain as a "once in a 100-year phenomenon," tilting the ship 60 degrees one way, then 40 degrees back. As a result, 62 containers were lost overboard about 20 miles off Land's End – and one of them was filled with nearly 4.8m pieces of Lego, bound for New York. No-one knows exactly what happened next, or even what was in the other 61 containers, but shortly after that some of those Lego pieces began washing up in both the north and south coasts of Cornwall. They're still coming in today. Since 1997, those pieces could have drifted 62,000 miles ... Theoretically, the pieces of Lego could keep going around the ocean for centuries.

American oceanographer Curtis Ebbesmeyer, commenting on the incident, summed up the sinister aspect of all this.

> The most profound lesson I've learned from the Lego story is that things that go to the bottom of the sea don't always stay there ... The incident is a perfect example of how even when inside a steel container, sunken items don't stay sunken. They can be carried around the world, seemingly randomly, but subject to the planet's currents and tides. Tracking currents is like tracking ghosts – you can't see them. You can only see where flotsam started and where it ended up.

Plastic simply does not go away. Giving your children a set of building bits made of this seemingly indestructible material is an investment in an unpredictable future you cannot want for them, if only because we still do not know how much damage to the planet has already occurred. I absolutely believe that we can prevent more damage, but we must change our buying patterns. I know that manufacturers only respond to demand. So if we stop demanding our right to buy junk, the entrepreneurs of the world will provide better alternatives.

I freely admit that small children will not appreciate some of the ideas I have outlined above for a YBN and beyond. Nothing says disappointment to a 6-year-old like a jar of organic mint jelly. But there are so many alternatives that *will* bring them equal joy and more creativity:

■ Books – thousands of choices.

■ Wooden blocks: give the assignment of coming up with a used set to someone who is Internet savvy, or make and paint (using toxin-free paint) your own.

■ Wooden beads and elastic: children can make their own bracelets and necklaces.

■ Paper, paints, and crayon sets: you don't have to buy them pre-fabricated; create your own.

■ Yarn and embroidery kits: Knitting Nancy is still around, though I am afraid that spool is plastic now, so substitute your own wooden one.

■ A gift basket for a teen, chock full of safe toiletries: young shavers can be coerced into better shaving habits with a brush and "clean" soap set. Girls will find the more sophisticated packaging of the new brands just as alluring as what the Big Boys offer.

■ Cooking lessons: our grandson thinks making jelly, cookies, and frosting cakes are all miracles. In winter we make "snowbet" (sherbet made of snow.) We add flavoured syrups or fruit (lemonade or OJ) concentrates to snow he collects himself, and whip it up with a whisk.

And that brings me to the gift of time. Most children would just love to spend time with you, right up and into their teens and beyond. For a birthday, plan a hike and make it a treasure hunt by pre-selecting a spot to seed with a candy or some other treat. Take a picnic with you on a bike ride. Come Christmas, give a pledge of a movie, concert, or play night to a youth. You can make your own nachos and watch a DVD at home, or go out to a venue and have hot chocolate after at a local hangout. By giving your time, you are building a relationship or strengthening an existing one.

I vividly recall going to see a movie with my mother's younger (and, I thought, very glamourous) sister. I was 14 and we lined up for something a little daring. Perhaps an Elvis Presley movie? Afterwards, I slept over at Auntie Renee's and she wowed me with a tour of her jewellery drawer. She had pop-beads, considered very daring at the time!

For youngsters of any age, don't be afraid to turn it up a notch on creativity. My father taught me to speed-read one summer on the beach, as a birthday present. I have had reason to bless this gift many, many times over in my life. My mother did not enjoy cooking, so I did my culinary training at Auntie Lil's house. No cute-cookie stuff for us! We'd make *choux* pastry, fill cabbage rolls, and stuff a turkey – with a chicken.

What Mum brought to the party was a sense of whimsy. She would stage a Dessert Supper, set out on the car rug on the living room floor on those occasional nights when my father had to work late. My sister and I would chow down on peanut butter and jelly sandwiches, fruit salad, milk pudding (made in kitchen mugs!), and oatmeal cookies. And Mum did not sit on the sidelines watching; she got right down there with us. My sister and I remember this as great fun many, many years later, and so will the young ones in your life.

Before you go thinking that all this sounds a little lame and could not possibly offer contemporary teens the buzz they've come to expect, let me reassure you. Within the last decade, I served as Don (housemother) to a residence of 50 teenage girls. My husband taught their male counterparts and they were just as needy, pathetically grateful for the taste of a homemade Caesar Salad at "boys night in." Underneath the makeup and the bravado, teens harbour uncertainty and a need for adult approval. Give them your time and your attention. You may be offering something they will treasure for life. And it's so much better than plastic doodads or another T-shirt.

■ This counter is closed: healthy alternatives to buying stuff

By now you will have realized that I have been a major shopper in my day. I might have substituted my lingerie craving for your shoe passion, or hoarding craft supplies for your addiction to real jewellery. I do know the thrill of the chase and, to a degree, this book likely reads like the true confessions of a reformed shopaholic. I believe I have broken the patterns of a lifetime and have lived to tell the tale. I do not want to sound smug about it as I am still enthralled by the need to acquire and am working hard to find appropriate substitutes. I truly believe that humans are hard-wired to bring home a harvest and must fight primal animal instincts to get past this addiction.

I have not read widely about the psychology of acquisition but I readily admit to the high I get from bringing home a load of bags or boxes of just about anything. I feel I am storing up treasure that will keep me safe. It is as if I am some ancient tribal matriarch putting away edibles against a threatened famine. If this latter feeling were limited to food supplies, it would make more sense. But I recognize the same satisfaction coming home with two giant containers of eco-friendly dish washing liquid that was on sale, no less! I saved $1.42! Why should this feel *so* good? What on earth do I need a three-year supply of dish suds for?

I have watched those shows on television that reveal the warehouse full of goods purchased by keeners who use an enormous amount of time and brain power to engineer supermarket trips fuelled solely with coupons. The big tally is sometimes merely peculiar, but more often shocking: 42 boxes of Skittles and a crate of Lucky Charms. Who could possibly view this as a good thing for a parent to have on hand? These shows strike me as just a shade of crazy away from the pathetic lives of hoarders revealed on the program that will likely follow on the same channel. We recognize this sort of behaviour as unhealthy. Too much is just too much!

At the same time, I admit I am not in a position to pass judgment on those who collect in appropriate ways. I have a collection of "fun" vintage tablecloths that earned their worth by bedecking the wedding feast at our daughter's marriage. That it was the only time they were ever *all* in use and that it might be the *only* time they ever will be does not prevent me from covetously eying "just one more" when I go to a yard sale. Tablecloths aren't the only things I have collected. I finally gave away the jade-ware collection that threatened to eat the kitchen; and I sold off a full set of wedding china – the second set, the "good china" that young couples were once induced to see as mandatory to a happy life?! I trust that's a concept from the past.

Yet I would dearly like to have on hand every mystery story I treasure, a full set of Sayers and P. D. James and Rankin and... Well, you get the picture. I know this is not rational. I know that I can, with very little effort, download what I want to read when I want to read it. Or since I still love the *feel* of a real book, I could borrow it from the library. I know I do not need to own these books, and yet...

I came by my need to over-buy honestly, along with the rest of my generation. We are the children of those who lived through the Depression. But recently, I have noticed I am definitely not alone in turning aside this pattern of behaviour. As we deal with the estates of our deceased parents, we are brought up short at the sheer magnitude of stuff we must either absorb into our own households, or discard, somehow. It can be painful, and we sense it is wasteful. There is no market now for second-hand furniture because it can be bought new so cheaply. And those fruit nappies and a full set of crystal stemware? More people than you might imagine no longer know what those things are.

So if with every fibre of your being you know you just can't buy more things and you still want to get that feeling that comes with having a full house, what are you to do? If you feel you cannot quit the mall cold turkey, try to confine your buying to antique stores and second-hand emporiums. Go window shopping at thrift stores and yard sales and second-hand bookstores. But do be aware that this is just an interim measure and you still have the addiction.

You can make the final step and live without needless buying, but you must substitute healthier activity. There is a group of people out there who are finding ways to sublimate their baser acquisitive instincts and to turn their hands and minds to something more productive instead. Actually *creating* something is key here, I think. In the process of researching this book, I have come to know many such people, of all ages and all demographics. There are bakers and cooks and those who preserve or can. There are gardeners, and thank God for those good people. There are writers and poets and playwrights and choristers and musicians and actors. There are knitters and sewers and crafters and quilters and hookers (no, not that kind – the kind that make rugs and stair treads and wall hangings). There are people who raise chickens and/or cows, or who go fishing. There are people who rescue dogs and cats; their creation is a new life for a fellow being. There are painters and sculptors and potters and bookbinders and woodworkers. There are folks who volunteer to visit the elderly and create happiness, or who raise money for breast-cancer research and thus extend life, or who build houses for Habitat for Humanity. All of these things represent truly productive effort. Every single one of these things is better for you and for the world than buying more perfume or another cute top, or another plastic "anything." Every single one of these things will take time that you might have spent buying stuff. And you will feel more worthy and *cleaner* after doing these things, or bringing them into your home, than you would have buying something from the mall, and that is a *very* good thing.

■ Part II

Vegetable

(but really, all things edible and potable)

■ Chapter 4

Food, Glorious Food!

■ A word about this part of the book

YOU MAY BE CURIOUS AS TO HOW I CAN JUSTIFY TAKING UP A BIG BITE OF THIS BOOK ON THINGS EDIBLE AND POTABLE, things I was legitimately able to purchase during my YBN. This is, after all, supposed to be a book about the impact of *buying nothing*. I could blame it on the spare time I had to think about food when I was freed from the preoccupation of so many other buying decisions. But the deeper truth is that this year made me drill down hard to understand what "environmentally friendly" really means when it comes to me and my family meal plan. This was part of a long educational process for me, since I was born in the 1950s when not being a polluter meant refraining from tossing litter out the car window.

Saving the planet is a good thing. In any referendum on the subject, we would surely vote "YES!" But what does the word "sustainability" look like when enacted in one's own kitchen? I didn't really know. I had at different times in my culinary life been mesmerized by manu-speak (what food producers tell you on the packages) and bamboozled by bio-babble (what advertisers claim). While I had gotten over that and was educated in reading a label as far as calorie count was concerned, I remained ignorant about what was going into my grocery cart. I have learned a lot. My education did not all come in the past 12 months, but I did put it all together this year. And I am ready to open my cupboards to your inspection and share whatever tips you may find useful.

■ A funny thing happened on the way to the cash register

Confession: food, in all its glorious manifestations, is my hobby. I bring the same enthusiasm to it and passion for it that a philatelist has for stamps, or an oenophile for wine.

I checked out sexy words to describe devotees of my hobby and got stuck with "gourmet" or "glutton." I am neither of those things. While I do enjoy the consumption part of this food thing, I am not particularly sophisticated in my tastes nor am I a ter-rifically big eater. We could settle for "foodie," but again, strict definitions for that hobby are more defined by the act of *eating*, whereas I like to buy, prep, grow, cook and serve food *almost* more than actually consuming it. I say, almost, because there really is nothing like a perfectly balanced Caesar salad, strewn artistically with a petite Getaway Farms' strip loin, followed by a blueberry tart. But we'll get to eating soon enough.

During the years I was involved in the magazine industry, cooking kept me humble and was my soother and my shrink. There is no better way to keep your feet on the ground and re-mind you that *you are not your job* like a big old chicken carcass waiting for you to dismantle it for stock. You can't beat kneading bread dough or mashing potatoes to take away the stress of the day. And there is nothing like hearing from your child that "Eliza-beth's mum makes all *their* pasta from scratch" to humble you and remind you that you remain an amateur in your own kitchen, even if you *do* sit on the Executive Committee at work.

When I semi-almost-not-really retired and moved to the coun-try four years back, I was determined to do food prep from the ground up, which for me meant the following: grow and pre-serve as much as I could, carefully source from local markets what I couldn't, eat in-season, consume only bread and baked goods that came from my own hands, and learn to make pasta like Elizabeth Russo's mama.

I did manage to fulfill *some* of these aspirations. I also learned that some things are beyond me if I am to keep on the pleasure side of the hobby-cooker charts. Some of those goals were sim-ply beyond my patience (pasta-making), skill and experience (not everything one plants in the ground, comes up from the ground, duh!) and time-constraints (shopping at the local market, which is only open on Thursdays). Life requires compromise, right?

But one thing I did have completely under control was our weekly budget. I knew our spending habits and could predict them, to the penny. We spent weekly, on average, $90 at the grocery store, $30 at the butchers and/or market, $15 for those last minute pick-ups of milk or butter or salsa. The total: $135 per week or about $7,000 per year.

This represents the expenditure for an *average* week and covers the consumption of two people every day, a youngster for two to three meals a week, afternoon tea for girlfriends, and a weekly "big" dinner for family or friends. We breakfast at home daily and take our lunches to work or eat at home pretty much every day. Naturally, there are periods that cost a lot more, weeks that include a major holiday like Easter or Christmas, or when visitors, happily, come and play on our porch in summer. But those times are balanced out by others when we find ourselves gorging solely from the garden, or vacation days when all consumption gets classified as "travel." Neither meals out, on holiday or otherwise, or takeout (monthly pizza) are included in that total.

So imagine my shock when one month into my YBN, instead of $135, I was averaging $*160* for weekly groceries. And this was *after* I removed all toiletries and paper and plastic products from my list. All logic dictated it should have been lower – quite a bit lower.

I looked closely at my pantry, fridge, and recent receipts for clues to this mysterious disappearance of cash.

The solution was staring me in the face (and would have shortly migrated to my hips): Triple Crème Cheese, two flavours of locally smoked salmon, Bacon Jam, a flat of Italian tuna-in-olive-oil, and three (yes, three!) jars of peach preserves with brandy. Hey, they were on special!

It seems that to counteract the purchasing "deprivation" I was experiencing, I had been unconsciously pantry-loading with expensive non-essential edibles. The total impact really *did* come as a surprise. And a wake-up call!

My theory is that by altering my buying trends, reducing what had become "normal" (i.e., the list that always included at least some plastic wrap, chemically-soaked cloths for the business end of my sweeping thingy, aluminum foil, bleach, nail polish, stain remover, and five sizes of freezer bags), I had "compensated" by creating a bulge in another area of my purchasing pattern. I have spoken already of the animal need to stock up that nest, as a basic instinct. I believe this was another manifestation of that.

My new overspending was easy to get a handle on. I simply took actual cash to the supermarket instead of my debit card, thus ensuring I spent to my list and my budget. No foodie flings, and less of the "what if the road doesn't get plowed and we *need* two jars of peanut butter" panic. Nipped that in the bud. But it was a good lesson for my YBN and for the rest of time.

■ Then and now-ish

The truth is that my food-buying habits were okay, but not great. I had come a long way from the days when as a kid I helped my mom carefully separate out the elements of the Kraft Dinner. If you lived through those years you will already know this: the 1950s were for most North American families, days of food naivety. In my Scottish-Canadian family, we did not know that pasta could be purchased any other way than in that box. When we needed macaroni for Mum's Famous Mucky Gutchie Casserole – 1 pound ground beef, 1 tin tomato soup, 1 cup cooked elbow noodles – we reached for the kit. We saved the "cheese" sauce packet for dressing up canned corn, for guests. (I did warn you that I do not come from a family of chefs!)

But that was then and this is now-ish. While I had developed some solid skills over the years between that day and December 31, the eve before the start of my YBN, I have come a lot further now, not perhaps in my food buying patterns *per se*, but in kitchen management for a healthier diet *and planet*.

Once upon a time, I scorned those who boasted of their penchant for organic fruits and vegetables. I bought on price and prided myself on the variety of menus I produced for a very low cost. While I enjoyed creating some involved recipes, I never worried about the provenance of the apples for my Pommes Galette or the spinach for my Saag Ghosh.

Then I read authors who had really researched the contemporary food industry and its agricultural underpinnings. Authors like Michael Pollan (*The Omnivore's Dilemma, The Botany of Desire*), Barbara Kingsolver (*Animal, Vegetable, Miracle*), Wendell Berry (*Our Only World, The Gift of Good, The Unsettling of America*), and Dan Barber (*The Third Plate*).

I got it. I read them all and was transformed. What followed was an evolution in my thinking and in my food-buying habits. Words like "sustainability" and "environmental conscience" started to become part of my vocabulary. Packaging became a factor. Previously, it had all been about interesting meals at a great price. Now I know there is a much more important bottom line than the one on any individual's bank statement.

If, as a consumer, I demand perfect-looking avocados at $1 each, in February, I am pretty much ensuring appalling growing and picking conditions, the waste of as much as one-third of the crop due to cosmetic "imperfections," and the racking up of tonnes of carbon emissions to get them to me from thousands of miles away. If I demand ground round at bargain-basement prices, I may get mega-doses of antibiotics as a side dish, and I almost surely condemn the animals involved to a wretched life and a grim death.

If I marvel at how anyone would go to the trouble of seasoning their own rice when "the maker of this little red box does it so cheaply," I am stacking up some very big losses indeed. Not in my budget, perhaps, but in the health of my family, in the bank balance of the local economy, and long-term, in regards to the very existence of human life on this planet. That little red box contains the cheapest possible rice. That means the fastest grown grains, most saturated in chemical fertilizers and pesticides. Rice that was probably picked under appalling conditions by people for whom a living wage remains an unobtainable dream. It contains "vegetables" so desiccated by chemical preservation they are pretty much indistinguishable from the "herbs and spices." The salt content has a number on it disclosing that even the tiny "suggested serving size" represents 37% of the daily maximum allowance. Then the entirety is soaked in unpronounceable preservatives so that it can remain shelf-stable forever. The resultant meal of Tex-Mex Beef & Rice? That's not dinner. That's an ethical and nutritional crime!

■ How I got this concerned about corn, confit, and consommé

I was always curious about food and meal preparation. My mother was *not* interested in cooking and had a strictly food-as-fuel approach in the kitchen. She was, however, most attentive about ensuring the family ate a decent breakfast of oatmeal, a simple-but-appropriate lunch, and she served up a "square meal" (meat, potato, and two vegetables) every night at supper. Simple grilled meat, boiled or roasted potato, and two vegetables (1 raw, 1 cooked), salt and pepper, and infrequently, butter or sauce. A piece of fruit for dessert, or if it was a weekend night, junket. Milk was the beverage for all, while grownups were additionally offered tea, strong and often. As it turns out, that is a very healthy way to ensure decent nutrition for a growing family and it kept everyone's weight in check.

It was my father who aspired to a more interesting plate. He loved the farmer's market, which was open only on Saturdays in a town 90 minutes away. We rose at 5:30 to be there before all the "good stuff" was gone. For my dad, who had been raised in Britain in the brief halcyon days between the wars, the good stuff included lamb, sausage, and rabbit; cheeses from France and Germany; squash, turnip, and chard; orchard fruits in season; and smelts, bass, and pickerel from local lakes. He would bring them home proudly and would enthusiastically supervise their preparation, with mother as dutiful sous-chef – not that either of them would have recognized the term.

I took over my mother's role as dicer and chopper as soon as I could wield a knife. When I insisted on knowing what made the chocolate pudding thicken, and the difference between a *soft-boiled* versus *coddled* egg, I was shuffled off to my "Auntie" Lil's for "real" cooking lessons. The first time, I was probably no older than eight. I recently spent a few days cooking side by side with Lil again. She taught me the version of the Grilled Portobello and Mustard Salad she'd adapted from the Food Network. Lil remains way ahead of me in culinary skill!

Auntie Lil and Uncle Fred were not relatives but good family friends. Lil was a kindergarten teacher and a creative and inspired cook, with a Ukrainian-Canadian background. She was deeply fond of my mother and openly enthusiastic about having me as her apprentice, as it gave her a chance to exercise two of her many great skills: she could both cook and teach!

Lil was way ahead of her time. When most cooks of the day were falling in love with "convenience foods," she had bookshelves of cookbooks and notebooks filled with ideas and sketches, and she loved to experiment. She had a freezer that yielded chicken, beef, and seafood pies, her own stock, and homemade ice cream. In her kitchen, there were two drawers of fascinating spices with exotic names, cupboards with pasta from sources other than a Kraft Dinner box, and a pantry with pickles, fruit, and jams she had "put up" herself. I got it. *This* could all be mine!

I was well and truly launched on a lifetime love affair with the care and feeding of the folks I care about. My personal cookbook collection remained fairly rudimentary however (*Betty Crocker's Cookbook for Boys and Girls* and *Carnation's Fun to Cook*), until the day that we went on a family trip to a re-created pioneer farm village. In the gift shop, I spied a cookbook that, while new, had a right to its place on the shelf as it spoke with the voice of the past. It was the *Farm Journal's Country Cookbook*, the 1959 edition.

I bought that book and spent hours poring over it. I plagued my family to look for others in the series. I think there were about 15 titles in all, published from this offshoot of the *Farm Journal Magazine*, which is still around today, after 134 years.

The tone was completely unselfconscious. The mission was to use produce that came directly from the farmer's field, and protein from the barn and henhouse. As was typical for the day, they provided excellent advice on canning and preserving, and took a no-nonsense approach to the occasional time-saving addition of a "store-bought" ingredient.

This is the quote from the *Farm Journal's Freezing and Canning Cookbook – 1963* that started me on a lifetime habit of big-batch cooking. It explains the thinking of an Ohio farm woman who especially likes to cook for her freezer in March: "Spring and summer are busy times. When I get off the tractor, milking demands my attention along with the hens – and supper! I have to get something hearty and tasty in a hurry, so I plan ahead and have frozen dinners on hand for jiffy use."

Something about that vision called to me then and still has meaning for me today. Me, the woman who has never actually touched a cow's udder, who has yet to ride a tractor, and who only very recently ever held a live chicken. *The Farm Journal* edition in which this Ohio farmer explains herself includes descriptions of how to render lard and how to take advantage of surplus cream yield. It extolls the virtues of using persimmons growing wild in the hedgerows, and teaches the best method to gut fish and to carve up that deer your brother dropped off. If they throw in a can of condensed cream of celery soup every once in a while, well, that is just practical!

I learned to cook like that, requesting a freezer as a 21st birthday gift and spending happy afternoons with girlfriends making a dozen pies, before heading out with a boyfriend to hit the smoke-filled coffee houses and folk clubs.

The first meal I ever prepared for my much-later-to-be-husband (then a classmate at university) was an end-of-term celebration for our seminar group, numbering about 8. I was confident enough to invite our professor and served Chicken Della Robbia. (There had been a reference to one of Andrea Della Robbia's sculptures in the Victorian poetry class.) I also bought, perhaps for the first time, a bottle of decent wine and in my insatiable curiosity to discover how the pretty gilt netting was affixed to the bottle, I turned it upside down. It was neither corked nor empty at the time. Perhaps this is a good moment to mention that I am accident prone?

■ Life of the working woman

Being hooked on big-batch cooking early was a huge asset when the busy years hit like a domestic hurricane. By the time our daughter arrived on the scene, I was a senior manager in the publishing industry. Time was money at work and at home, more precious than gold. Those Auntie-Lil-inspired pies jammed with veggies and beef, fish or chicken, combined easily with a salad for a family weeknight meal. I made up gallons of sauce from market tomatoes on a Sunday afternoon, placed it in the freezer and converted it to pasta sauce, and bases for soups and casseroles of all descriptions. When I cooked a roast for a dinner party, I popped two in the oven and cut up the extra chicken, beef, or ham for curries, shepherd's pie, stir-fried rice. There was bread dough and the base for fruit crisps in the freezer, too. And, like the gal in the *Farm Journal* cookbook, I had freezer preserves tucked away in there, too: applesauce, raspberry coulis, and strawberry-rhubarb preserves.

Now, I hasten to add, I did not do all this on my own. The planning may have been mine, but my mother lived with us from the time our daughter was born, and though she always remained disinterested in the process, Mum could be counted upon to prep potatoes, salads, and fruits. My husband was Mr. Reliable when it came to picking up that last-minute item on his way home from work. And we took turns in the kitchen, especially on weekends. Even though I had to return to my briefcase after dinner hour, I took it as a personal challenge to be present at the family table as many weeknights as I could. We were much luckier than most two-career families. Due to organization and cooperation, we ate together and at a table set with home-cooked meals on most nights.

This family-eats-together-ethic was an extended-family thing that reached beyond our own home and into that of my husband's sister and her family, with whom we were very close, and to my in-laws as well. We frequently ate at each other's houses on weekends, swimming in their above-ground pool in summer and playing board games and cards in winter, laughing our heads off and enjoying our children who grew up together and who remain close. That my sister-in-law had married an Italian only cemented the family-food-love relationship.

Of all the things I have accomplished in this life, this is among the most important to me. From the time our daughter was old enough for it to be a question, she knew she could ask home whomever she wanted, but on Sunday nights we had a date to be together around a family dinner table. She conducts her own household in the same manner today – when they are not here at our table, of course!

■ So where did I go wrong?

My spare time was eaten by the increasing demands of my career. There were evenings that had to be devoted to entertaining clients – and some not-so-entertaining ones! The Sunday afternoons I had treasured as big-batch cooking time got swallowed up in children's birthday parties, Brownie tests, and ballet and piano recitals. I freely admit that as time became tighter, I increasingly relied on the addition of "a can of this" or "a package of that" to take my ingredients from a line of stuff sitting on the counter, through to delicious. That Mucky Gutchie recipe (I use the term "recipe" loosely), which I quoted above, the one that was my mother's first foray into noodle casseroles? That was a family favourite in *our* house, too, and it started to appear more frequently (I had figured out where to buy pasta!). Way too many of my meals became dependent on the addition of those magic red-and-white tins of soup. I harboured a real affection for recipes called Spanish Chicken Supreme, Turkey Divine, and Jelly-Crème Surprise. They were prominently featured on the packages of prepared ingredients neatly lined up in my cupboard, and in the ads for all those packaged-goods manu-facturers.

Except for a once-a-month Friday pizza-and-pyjamas-video-night, we were never much into takeout foods. Neither my husband nor I enjoyed the fare at the chains that increasingly lined suburban motorways. But I am in no position to boast, as I freely admit I did cheat a lot with things like frozen chicken fingers and fish sticks to "anchor" meals. Though I knew better, I started to rely on guacamole and macaroni "salads" from plastic containers. The packets that made chili easier replaced *my* homemade spice mix. And when food prep "advanced" to the point where pre-cut lettuce came in a bag, washed and ready to add the bits that came in cellophane pouches and the pouch of dressing, I was hooked. For about three years, I pretty much abandoned anything green that wasn't salad from a bag.

Why was this such a problem? Especially if most meals were still based on fruits and vegetables and meats and fish that *did* come fresh? Was it reprehensible to "bind" them into interesting combinations with packaged mixes?

The answer is yes, it was – and not just because if Auntie Lil had found out she'd have quartered me like a chicken. Most of those items that I was using to "enhance" our meals are saturated with salt, sugar, hydrogenized fats, and preservatives. They are as unrelated to real food as video games are to stage plays. What you find in those convenient mixes simply *isn't* good nutrition.

And then there is the word *package*. When you buy a chicken, some lemons, and garlic to roast and serve with rice and a salad, the impact on the landfill is basically *nil*. If your chicken comes from a butcher, you can recycle the paper it was wrapped in. The lemons, garlic, and salad fixings can be purchased without unnecessary plastic and, if you remember the re-usable grocery sacks or bags (and, of course, you do!), you can skip that bag, too. The spices for the rice come from clever little glass bottles or tins that last forever and can be refilled from spice purveyors.

The rice comes in large containers and you can buy it in bulk, thus eliminating that box.

If, however, you go the "convenience" route and buy Freezer Delight Lemon Garlic Chicken, Dolly Eastern Salad (in a plastic shell), and Samaritan Packaged Ricearina, you are likely adding a minimum of two boxes, a plastic sheet from the plastic freezer container, as well as the container itself, a plastic "shell" from the salad, as well as two to three cellophane/plastic envelopes of additions, and a plasticized inner wrap or two from the rice mix – all of which goes into that landfill. It adds up.

Another negative is the dietary aspect. The salt content, the added processed sugars in both the chicken meal and the pre-mixed salad, the hydrogenated and trans-fats, the preservatives in all the components – these are largely avoidable with home-cooked meals. Not so with packages. That adds to the cumulative intake of bad things for your family diet.

And then there is the issue of the unknown sources. When I buy a chicken at my local purveyor of poultry, I know how it was raised. While much fun has been made of the *Portlandia* approach (and I hasten to assure you, I do not actually know the names of the chickens I buy), I *do* know how they were raised. They were not mass-produced like widgets in a chicken factory and salvaged from early death only by repeated doses of antibiotics. They came from down the road and I know what they ate, because the chap or gal who sold them to me picked them up fresh from the farm and knows the person who fed them.

The salad greens? When I buy a head of lettuce and some loose carrots and a cucumber, especially when I source organic produce, I know they have not been soaked in preservatives with the potential of added listeria (a nasty illness increasingly found in pre-washed mixed salads packs).

I leave it to you to figure out the potential threat-of-the-week. The media loves to shock us with the latest horror story of carcinogen-laced baby formula or salmonella-showered tomatoes. I know they mean well. Some of my best friends are journalists! And they want us to know what we are eating. But the problem is that it all starts to sound the same and the shock value is diminished. With each news item, instead of being horrified we become inured.

As I write this, there is a big story about a Monsanto product called Round-Up in the news. It contains something called glyphosate, a chemical herbicide (weedkiller). It also appears to induce cancer in humans, according to the International Agency for Research on Cancer study released in March 2015. Let me state clearly that I don't know if glyphosate is or is not dangerous to humans, and at what concentrate it goes from benign to lethal. I *do* know that provincial regulators in Ontario, Prince Edward Island, and New Brunswick are concerned enough to forbid sales in their regions. The controversy will carry on around us. I once would have sighed at the lunatic fringe who rail against the big chemical companies. But based on my reading, I can't afford to turn away from this information.

Through all of this I had wandered far from my vision of that Ohio farmwoman, leaping down from her tractor, chicken feed in one hand and receipt box in the other. But, bless her heart, she was increasingly part of a larger problem than my own, as her own small-hold farm operation got swallowed up by an agricultural conglomerate.

■ Salvation by the page

It was as a result of one-too-many scary stories of this sort (and hiding my dependency on Meal-in-a-Box from Auntie Lil) that I sought to rescue my family's meal plan from death-by-preservative. I was lucky as it was the early '90s and I was not alone in my plight. I was, however, uniquely blessed as I worked with one of the best test-kitchens on the continent.

The *Chatelaine* sections about all things edible were then under the inspired and capable direction of food editor Monda Rosenberg. This knowledgeable, practical, and very witty woman had helped me out of many a dinner party dilemma before. This time we sat down and talked about how women like us, balancing careers and family responsibilities, could adapt. Some were single, some married. But even with supportive partners such as my own, we were increasingly swamped with scheduling issues. Most of us had been brought up by stay-at-home moms who planned meals and cooked. Most of us had some culinary skills ourselves.

By the late 1980s, two things had occurred in the lives of women born in the '50s and '60s. We were active participants in the workforce in unprecedented numbers and the demands related to what goes on the table became increasingly complex. The simple square meal of my mother's dinner hour was neglected in favour of increasingly sophisticated flavours. When your restaurant options include Szechuan, Indian, Northern and Southern Italian, Portuguese and Ethiopian, to plonk a plain grilled chop on the plate with a boiled potato and steamed carrots doesn't measure up. Increasingly, when the rubber hit the road time wise, it was tempting to just head for takeout. This was also the day of the massive expansion of those golden arches and all the clones. Suppertime saw us guiltily packing up our cars with kids and heading for the easiest and fastest possible caloric gorge.

Monda Rosenberg and the team fought back with, first, *The New Chatelaine Cookbook* ("No-fuss recipes for family and friends") and, later, a cookbook series that was adapted from the pages of the magazine itself: *Quickies.* Both were very successful. While magazine competitors still seemed to be addressing full-time homemakers and offered up ingredient lists that took up half a page, Monda was serving up ideas that introduced ethnic diversity, included both old favourites and new protein options, and made vegetables interesting. And she completely understood the time pressures contemporary cooks were under, because she was one of us! I can think of no better example of her creative wizardry than this gem from *The New Chatelaine Cookbook*: the "One-Hour Sunday Roast." It had five ingredients, simple instructions, sane demands on the cook's time. The page included suggestions for sides that were innovative and easy to prepare: "Roasted Sweet Peppers" and "Wild Rice with a

Hint of Horseradish." It even had a sidebar that explained what green peppercorns are and how to use them. And not a box or plastic bag in sight.

Now, I recognize that all you folks born after 1970 know all about unripened peppercorns and roasting vegetables, but it was all new and heady stuff back in the early '90s. As was the idea that among the skill sets the average woman should be equipped with, along with computer savvy, managerial acumen and fashion finesse, was the trick of getting a meal on the table *fast*. *Superwomen*: I don't think so! But darn, we tried hard!

It was not Monda alone who saved the day in my kitchen. Others increasingly followed suit, and the words "super-fast" began to appear in recipes and on ads that did not simply extol the virtues of another freezer product.

Eventually, I did get back on track. I had to let go of some burdensome expectations of self, coming home and effortlessly whipping up 15-ingredient delights every night of the week.

By the time I had weaned myself from my addiction to convenience foods, I thought I had learned it all.

But I was careless enough to give birth to a child who later studied at a university with progressive ideas. I was foolish enough to have friends who thought long and hard about the environmental impact of how things are grown, and about the bodily impact of the dreck that they are increasingly grown in. They loaned me books. I borrowed books from the library. I got savvy. I got scared. I got smart.

■ Redefining "convenience"

The number one thing I learned is that "convenience" for me could mean massive potential inconvenience, like death, for many eco-systems and species, including our own. How would that manifest itself? Choking our soil to death with pesticides that are almost certainly carcinogenic. Stuffing plastic into the throats of our landfills, until they gag and spew their poisons over arable land. Dirty-driving produce thousands of miles to grace a table out of season. Overdosing animals (for human consumption) with antibiotics and hormones so *they* don't get sick, but when *we* do *we* have nothing to fight back with.

Sustainability begins at home, that is why keeping an ecologically healthy home is vital to your future and that of the planet. There is no choice. If you want to be a responsible, caring citizen of the globe, you simply have to take a stand and make wise choices. You must read the fine print on the label, not just the big *green* word, "healthy." Food manufacturers are not monsters, but they do live in a world driven mad by the need to increase profits. And you, the consumer, hold the true power here. Being knowledgeable is not that hard. And if you stop buying it, they will stop selling it. Believe me, if I can do it, anyone can!

■ "But have you seen the price of organic celery?"

Yes, organic produce does cost more. Yes, grass-fed beef and local free-range eggs are pricier than the other kinds. This is true. Believe me, I have wrestled with this one, granddaughter of that thrifty Aberdonian Scot that I am. It was a journey. I now have a working strategy to make "cleaner" grocery choices that lead to a sustainable kitchen *and* maintain a budget.

First, let me share an invaluable tool for buying produce. It is a list produced on an annual basis by the U.S. Department of Agriculture and the Food and Drug Administration Environmental Working Group (EWG). It has been widely quoted and subdivided into the Dirty Dozen (a different list entirely from the David Suzuki Foundation's Dirty Dozen list of personal care product ingredients) and the Clean Fifteen. The EWG has been checking the levels of pesticide in products since 2004.

Please understand when I say that the pesticides are in the products, not on them. Most commercial non-organic vegetables and fruits are grown on factory farms in soil that is heavily laced with fertilizers, herbicides, and pesticides. These toxins do not wash off.

Here is the full list of the produce most highly doused with pesticides, not just the top 12, from 2015, presented in order of greatest saturation of pesticides to least. (Note: I carry the one from 2008 in my purse at all times. The order has changed very little overall, so don't be overly concerned about having the most recent copy.)

1. apples
2. peaches
3. nectarines
4. strawberries
5. grapes
6. celery
7. spinach
8. sweet bell peppers
9. cucumber
10. cherry tomatoes
11. snap peas – imported
12. potatoes
13. hot peppers
14. blueberries-domestic
15. lettuce
16. kale/collard greens etc.
17. cherries
18. plums
19. pears
20. green beans
21. raspberries
22. winter squash
23. tangerines
24. blueberries – imported
25. carrots
26. summer squash
27. broccoli
28. snap peas – domestic
29. green onions
30. bananas
31. oranges
32. tomatoes
33. watermelon
34. honeydew melon
35. mushrooms
36. sweet potatoes
37. cauliflower
38. cantaloupe
39. grapefruit
40. eggplant
41. kiwi
42. papayas
43. mangoes
44. asparagus
45. onions
46. sweet peas – frozen
47. cabbages
48. pineapples
49. sweet corn
50. avocadoes

So how to use this list?

First, how do you go about finding produce that is not laced with pesticides? Look for the word "organic." It may be directly on the produce on a small light purple sticker, or on the grocery card-stock sign that has the price, or on the plastic wrapping or shell in which the item comes. You can trust this word on food products (unlike the words "healthy" or "natural," which mean whatever the manufacturer would like you to imagine they mean).

The word "organic" has a government-approved definition: it is a term given only to foods produced utilizing organic farming practices, and growth-enhancing products that are proven healthy both for you and the soil in which the produce is grown. There are slightly different standards worldwide. In North America, organic farming avoids the use of synthetic pesticides (some approved organic ones, such as fish-byproducts, may be used). Likewise chemical fertilizers are not permitted. Overall, organic farming fosters biological and mechanical practices that ensure cycling of resources and that promote "ecological balance, and conserve biodiversity" according to Wikipedia. (Note that Canadian "organic" labelling does not exclude Genetically Modified Organisms or GMOs, because Canadian laws do not enforce GMO labelling. I am not going to discuss GMOs here; it would be a whole other book!)

Foods labelled organic are not processed using irradiation either, if this is a concern for you. Producers in both Canada and the U.S. are strictly regulated and must obtain special certification by the Canadian Food Inspection Agency (CFIA) or the U.S. Department of Agriculture (USDA). The Canadian and American governments have agreements in place to assure cross-border safety of produce. They also monitor items labelled "organic" that come in from other countries, which are certified to comply with our government standards.

In our home (and in my opinion), not everything purchased must be organic and I use that EWG list strategically.

∎ I *never* buy apples or potatoes that are not organic. (Nor would I buy apple- or potato-based products not labelled organic: e.g., bottled applesauce, candy apples on a stick, boxed scalloped potatoes, deli potato salad.) My reasoning for those two? Apples because I have seen how pesticide-soaked they are for myself, and potatoes because they spend so long in chemically altered soil. Also, I can grow both those items myself (see Chapter 5, "Grow Your Own").

■ I *rarely* buy anything else from the top 12 (*The Dirty Dozen*) that is not labelled organic and, if I do, I buy very small amounts and would never serve them to children.

■ I will *freely* buy items that come from the bottom 15 (*The Clean Fifteen*) without checking the labels. Consuming non-organic onions, for instance, does not trouble me

■ For the items in the middle (i.e., numbers 13–35), my rule is to seek out organics. If the price does not make me faint, I *prefer* to purchase produce with that purple label. If I cannot find, for example, organic green onions (#29), I will substitute cooking onions (#45) or do without, or use the least amount I can possibly get away with.

That's really it when it comes to organic produce. Shopping in this way is not that hard. I became accustomed to using the lists within weeks of our daughter sharing her copy with me about eight years ago. Now they are simply part of my buying pattern. As far as packaged products are concerned, I seek out items that are organic and purchase them as I can afford them, again using the list. So, for example, I will buy regular pineapples (#48 on the list) in a can for my husband's favourite cake. But I would not purchase peaches (#2) in a can that is not labeled organic.

Not all food purchases are made in grocery stores and somehow we have the trusting notion that farm markets are a superior venue. Sometimes they are. But it depends entirely on the oversight or management of the individual market operator. Regulation can be very slack. Local purchase does not guarantee that produce was treated in a chemically clean, sustainable manner. I have also seen some jiggery-pokery practised at so-called "local" stalls. Sometimes that produce is not from anywhere remotely local, but was purchased in bulk at the supermarket and cunningly arranged to look earthy and homey. Don't assume produce is organically and responsibly grown unless it says so.

Roadside stands can also be problematical. Where I live, blueberries are grown and sold in season where every farm field meets the road. I do not buy them unless I know that they came from one of the few landholds where the growing practices are environmentally above-board. As a result, I pay twice what my neighbours pay. But as I have personally observed the spraying process in a non-organic blueberry field, seen the protective gear the workers wear, watched the toxic mist get on everything, and felt its bite in my throat, I'd rather pay than eat spray.

To be clear, farmer's markets and roadside stands can be fine and I like the sense of knowing the folks that grow my food. My advice is simply to be a bit wary of farmers' markets and roadside stands that you do not know well. Otherwise, I agree that local is better in many ways. It serves the economic needs of your neighbours and it suggests that you are buying in-season, which means you are not paying the carbon-emission price of long-distance shipping by truck (or ship, or plane).

■ Beyond produce

What about packaged products? Do you have to look for organic everything? I work hard to limit family consumption of packaged goods today. But a lot of things are staples, like flour and sugar, and a pretty fixed part of cooking patterns, and it is hard to be picky about every single thing that comes into your home right out of the gate. So I try to exercise common sense.

But I do buy organic flour, for instance. The story of wheat in this land is a fascinating one. Did you know that wheat is not an annual, but a perennial in its unaltered state? Dan Barber's *The Third Plate* tells the story and shows photos of real wheat plants with roots 20 feet long. They are what held the prairie soil in place before the day of the massive farms. The elimination of this plant and resultant soil erosion from those provinces and states is one of the primary factors that created the dust bowl conditions of the 1930s. Even though organic flour is pricey, I make my own bread (love that bread machine!) so the costs kind of average out.

I also stick to organic rice and I use my own spices to flavour that all-important dish in my family's meal-plan. (Full disclosure: I neither know nor care whether spices and herbs are organically grown, with the exception of basil for pesto, which I grow myself. The amounts of other herbs I use are minute. If someone made a convincing argument for why I should get picky about organic spices and herbs and I knew a source, I would likely make that part of my buying pattern, too.) Homemade stock and a few grounds of pepper and a pinch of cumin are better than any boxed rice mix and I can control the salt. Organic rice of just about any variety is easily sourced and seems to me to taste better.

Personally, I have not seen the necessity for organic sugar; but our daughter, a savvy shopper, uses *only* that organic variety. We don't use a lot of sugar, maybe two or three pounds a year, substituting maple syrup and honey. The syrup is local, harvested from trees in the area and it is not adulterated. Honey is a different matter entirely. It is a scandal what passes for honey on supermarket shelves these days. Recent tests have revealed high levels of adulterated product. There were trace amounts of actual honey, yes, but the rest of the viscous golden liquid was corn syrup, or diluted molasses, or other fake honey-like substances. Knowing this, I have vowed to only purchase local organic honey and, yes, it is worth it.

Staples also include the full range of dairy products. As Canadians, we are blessed by decisions taken by our government back in the 1990s. In general, growth hormones to stimulate milk production in dairy cows are not permitted for use in Canada. Canadian herds are not fed rBST (recombinant bovine somatotropin), a type of artificial growth hormone that increases milk production. Policies also demand that if a dairy cow is being treated for an illness and is taking antibiotics, she is temporarily removed from the milk producing herd and her milk is discarded. This keeps our milk flowing pure(r). This also means that no cheese or yogurt produced in Canada contains these added hormones.

The decision to ban rBST was not taken in the U.S. When we vacation there, I only buy organic products. Fond as I am of many of them, we avoid American cheeses and other items that are not clearly labelled organic. As a cheese fancier, I am grateful that there are more and more hormone-free cheeses every year from artisanal producers throughout the world.

I really enjoy making soup from scratch; it tastes so much better than canned. (I have one exception. I always have a can of that ubiquitous red-and-white Cream of Tomato soup on hand. It is the star ingredient in Mum's Famous Mucky Gutchie, and my own best comfort food. I just can't replicate it and believe me, I have tried.) Homemade soup also freezes brilliantly, so that's a slam dunk. Making soup is an excellent way to use up all the cooked bits a week of meal-making leaves languishing on the shelves of your fridge. My Aunt Lil taught me a really useful trick for this. All that vegetable water that usually gets poured down the kitchen sink when you drain carrots, peas, or potatoes makes excellent stock for soup. Just keep a quart container in your fridge for the Saturday soup pot. Lil froze quarts at a time for occasions when she felt like making quantities of soup. And as an added bonus, this is a really good way to eliminate our propensity to salt every bit of water we cook in. I know old cookbooks insisted on salted water, but it really is not necessary. And avoiding added salt has major health benefits.

Pasta dishes? Absolutely the best method to use up bits of roast anything, and then you can add leftover uncooked veggies. Why would I buy a box that then forces me to buy something else ("just add one pound of ground round and a tin of tomatoes")? Or a freezer version that costs $6 for $2 worth of ingredients?

I have already confessed that my pasta maker is very underutilized, even though it could be used to craft organic pasta (or more accurately, pasta from organic flour). When you can purchase dried pasta in every possible shape, organic and otherwise; and gluten-free pasta has become so much more palatable; and fresh pasta is available in every really big supermarket, it is hard to justify handmade. Having said that, on the few occasions I *have* made my own lasagna noodles or gnocchi or prepped ravioli for filling with squash, which I slather with sage butter, for a "big deal" dinner, it is worth the effort.

Yes, I am concerned about how wheat is grown and as the mother of a daughter with celiac disease (non-wheat consumption is essential), I am very much aware that commercially grown wheat-based flour is in everything. For my daughter and for those who must follow gluten-free diets, there are corn-based, bean-based, and rice-based flours, and there are packaged pasta and bread products available. Sometimes these are both organic and gluten-free. You may of course suffer some sticker shock. But, hey, it's whole oat-flake oatmeal or fava bean flour. You can justify $5 for a small package, because you are going to use it sparingly.

Of course, despite how all this may sound, I am far from being a saint in the kitchen. As a family, we *try* to only consume bread and baked goods that we make ourselves and my beloved bread machine helps a lot. But when time gets tight, we, too, opt for culinary hell-in-a-grocery-cart. For example, shortly before Easter, I made three loaves of bread: one cheese, one nut-and-seed, and one organic multi-grain. I baked a whole-wheat "knobby" (peel-on) apple cake with local maple syrup.

But the following week, just prior to Holy Week, my resolution to bake our bread went weak at the knees, as the church computer crashed just prior to three worship services, times two churches. The kitchen was the last place I wanted to be and some mighty sins happened there. Store-bought pecan pie appeared and disappeared in short order. I made grilled cheese sandwiches *twice* for supper from a loaf that I grabbed on the way home. I spotted a local, non-organic bakery French stick on the counter and was about to remonstrate with my husband. Then he made croutons for his World Famous Caesar Salad (so-named years ago by the international cohort of students we taught and fed at the high school in Italy, which I mentioned earlier). Me? I asked no questions. I just munched happily and distractedly away on food made by somebody else.

And again, what about the price of organic celery (the non-organic kind being one of the Dirty Dozen)? As I admitted earlier, it *is* more expensive than the other kind. Today, very early spring in my small town grocery store, the organic variety was $3.49. The regular was $2.79 for comparably-sized portions, a difference of 70 cents. Yes, that would add up if I bought celery every week. So I don't. It is as simple as that. Instead, I make a list before I shop, but I try to be flexible. If the price differential gets too great, say twice as much, I switch to something else green and crunchy and organic: like green onions from the middle of the list, or cabbage from the Clean Fifteen, where it truly doesn't matter.

And I use things up. Once upon a time, I grabbed celery, cut off the end, disposed of it, and put the celery stocks into a water-filled container in the fridge. Mid-week, they migrated to the back and perished. When they re-emerged, limp and pale, I tossed them.

Nowadays, organic celery gets the respect it deserves. As I buy it (and I try to do this mostly in-season), I plan how it will get used: chopped in a soup base, cut on the bias for stir fries, in a relish tray prepped and ready to go along with the carrots (a quick munch for dieters that's guilt-free). And that end I used to toss? It's a great addition to stock. The feathery celery leaves do well in a salad or stew. And when the stalks do get a tad tired, standing there in the used-to-be-yoghurt-container, I use them for braising in chicken broth and white wine. If I was truly inspired, I could then use the braising liquid to enrich a white sauce and gratinée with Swiss cheese to embellish the celery even further. This treatment is based on a dish I ate on New Year's Eve in a very fancy restaurant in the old part of Quebec City. I was so excited about that celery I nearly missed the *l'entrecote de boeuf* it accompanied. My point is that you can make $3.49 go a long way, if you really care about that veg!

■ Up next

I still need to discuss the meat and fish question (and dairy and eggs, too, although I have already touched on dairy). I will tackle those thorny animal-based consumption patterns shortly, but first I want to share the number-one tip for easier pesticide-and-other-toxin-free produce sourcing first. So let me take you someplace green.

■ Chapter 5

Grow Your Own!

THERE WAS A TIME, BACK IN THE 1960S, WHEN THAT PHRASE MEANT SOMETHING ELSE ENTIRELY. So I hasten to say that I am talking about fruits, berries, herbs, and vegetables. If you have a patch of sun, you can grow *something* and anything is better than nothing.

I am not much on flowers, though I am partial to marigolds, peonies, and *rosa rugosa,* the robust varietal of wild roses you see growing by the ocean (and in my yard). When we moved to our present home, I inherited a rose bed with a lot of finicky hybrids. I have replaced them individually as they inevitably perished from our "freeze-and-thaw-repeat" winters. I am fond of the members of the "Explorer" series of Canadian roses, a hardy collection based on the *rugosa* strain. There were peonies, too, in that inherited garden, which I have split, doubled, and quadrupled in number. My wonderful neighbour, Nellie, gave me lungwort (*pulmonaria*) and primroses (*primula vulgaris*). But that is it. My mantra is, if you can't eat it, it's not worth the effort. Plus we have deer, and when you have deer you can't really grow anything deer eat. And deer eat everything, I have discovered. Except those five things listed above – and the only reason they don't consume the roses is because of the clever recessed design of the bed and the scary mirrored globe that adorns it. That is the sum total of the flower advice you will get from me. Peonies and roses and marigolds all look okay in a vase (not together!), and in my opinion that's the only stuff you should ever put in a vase – things that come from a garden you know personally.

But garden edibles: that is an heirloom tomato of a different colour entirely. There are a million books out there that will dole out expert advice and extol the virtues of organic growing much more elegantly and eloquently than ever I could, so I will cut to the chase and share what I have learned. The big rules are easy.

1. To avoid pre-soaking in fungicides, herbicides, and pesticides, ensure everything you grow is grown from organic seed or seedling plants. This is easiest to do if you share with a reputable source, or buy your seedlings from a nursery you know well.

2. Don't grow vegetables you don't want to eat and wouldn't purchase at the store. If you think this rule doesn't get broken, look at all the zucchini folks try to foist on you every August, though admittedly that often has as much to do with overabundance as it does with dislike of the produce!

3. Don't grow too much of anything you don't want to or can't preserve, like radishes, for example. And zucchini (see #2).

4. Grow items from the Dirty Dozen list (see page 117) and you will avoid the high price of buying market organics.

5. For produce from beyond the Dirty Dozen, especially from among the Clean Fifteen, pick those items to grow that are pricey to buy. For example, there is no greater household economy than an asparagus bed planted from (organic) seed. That seed packet likely costs less than *one* bunch of in-season asparagus. Even a 4' x 6' plot will yield enough for a family of four, with enough left over for giveaways. The bed will last a century if carefully tended and you will drool at the sight of that first spear appearing in spring (but only if you love asparagus, see #2).

For vegetables, we currently grow asparagus, beets, cabbage, cucumbers, fava and French beans, kale (but don't tell my husband – he claims he doesn't care for kale so I harvest it very young and pass it off as spinach), four kinds of lettuce, potatoes (both Russet and "bakers"), several varieties of summer and winter squash, tomatoes (Black Krim, San Marzano, Gardener's Sweetheart Cherry, Mortgage Lifter, Pink Berkely Tie-dye), and tomatillo (the bees love them, and so do I for *salsa verde*).

Let's back up to those beets I just mentioned. Beets, along with a number of other vegetables and fruits, are not on the USDA EWG list, but are pesticide-drenched, according to a good site for information on items beyond the EWG list. Check out the "Food That's Safe to Eat" thread at WaterWorksValley.com.

Where was I? Oh yes. Paving the way to this ever-evolving list, I tried artichokes (I know, this is Canada not Cairo), broccoli, Brussel sprouts, cauliflower, celery, fennel, garlic, leeks, and peas. Remember what I said? Some stuff probably just won't work in your area (for me that's fennel) and some may just be too fussy in the growing or post-harvest prep for what you eventually end up eating (for me that would be peas). Don't waste a lot of time amending your earth and building clever cloches, and making yourself crazy with homemade organic pesticide sprays and "teas." Just grow what you and your soil and your zone like.

Both raspberries and blackberries grow wild at the edge of our property and we pick them with our grandson and make all kinds of dishes in the kitchen, including our own ersatz *cassis* for Kir Royale. The real stuff is made with blackcurrants and they grow on trees not bushes, but then we did not use real champagne either, but Prosecco. Whatever! It sure made Christmas brunch fun.

After several seasons of experimentation, I finally got the rhubarb and the bush blueberries in the right spot last year and I *think* we should see decent yields. I may experiment with a strawberry bed as those gorgeous berries are among the most toxic in their un-organic state and organic ones are gone from the local farm market before I get there. "Grow your own," the helpful woman suggested when I remarked on how fast they disappeared.

For herbs, I grow basil (lots of it tucked all around the feet of the toms, to make pesto), chives, mint, summer savoury, sage, and parsley. Wild thyme grows...well, wild. I once gave lots of space in the herb garden to lavender. It is woody and pushy and needs finicky pruning and when I thought about it, I let it go. I don't "get" lavender as a flavouring for ice cream, and jam etc. It tastes like soap to me. A good gardener learns how to prune out items that don't earn their keep.

We also have fruit trees: two kinds of cherry, one sour and one sweet. They are a work-in-progress. Last year, four seasons after the initial planting, we had six cherries. You read that right – *six cherries*. Sure, they tasted good, but six? Those trees seem plagued. The sweet varietal hit a PVC drain pipe underground during its initial planting and caused a flood in our basement. It has since been relocated and has survived, so full marks for hardiness. The other became deer fodder and then got some kind of disease from the dampness of the summer and split. It needed to be cut back so dramatically, it is now shorter than when we first planted it four years ago. They are like two little wood-warriors, not at all the glorious pair in my mind's eye when planted, but so brave. Even if they don't produce cherries, they may be allowed to remain as ornamentals, a testimony to the survival spirit in the wood.

On the other hand, we have a crabapple and two Mcintoshes that languished ignored since the days 40 years ago when this area was orchard. Today, that beautiful crab yields a generous and dependable harvest each year, after its assiduous pruning. I am modestly well-known locally for my spiced crabapple jelly (okay, both my neighbours like it). The Mac's will revive. After years of neglect, and under my husband's tender ministrations and the tutelage of YouTube videos, there was a decent apple crop last year.

Bottom line: I am not a clever gardener. I resist advice and like to do it by myself. Even If I fail, I enjoy the process. But the meanest talent for domestic economy suggests that the work involved in doing it my way or the *proper* way (where you actually read books, test and amend your soil, check out websites, belong to garden clubs, and listen to other people's advice *and then take it*), well, either way, it is really, really worth it. *You* control the toxins and even organic seeds are dirt-cheap.

And don't feel you can't do this if you don't have a big garden plot, or your garden faces the wrong direction and light is an issue. There are terribly intelligent people who will tell you how to grow herbs on your window sill and tomatoes on your balcony and spinach in the shade. Look them up and *grow your own!*

■ The seedy side of my YBN

Notice anything missing in my original YBN planning? I forgot all about the garden. It just simply slipped my mind, sitting at my desk in the depths of winter. I do maintain a line in our annual household budget for the yard, but I was focussed on items like getting the drive plowed after a snowstorm and only budgeted that for my YBN, completely ignoring the necessity of acquiring seeds, fertilizer, gardening tools, etc. Which is weird, because I *did* make the conscious decision *not* to purchase roses. But that's the fallibility of the human brain. A computer would have prompted me.

When seed-planting time arrived in mid-March, I was flummoxed at first. I did have a limited number of viable seeds to trade, something folks do increasingly here, both formally (at Seedy Saturdays) and casually with neighbours. I had beet and fava bean and basil seeds and some mixed mesclun lettuce, but nothing else. I had to improvise the rest.

My first tactic was whining. Yes, I am not above begging when it might prove useful for feeding my family. This worked well. My tender-hearted daughter had leftover tomato and cucumber seeds and handed them right over. My gardening-mad girlfriend was made of sterner stuff and bartered with me: a batch of oatmeal shortbreads in exchange for a fling at the local seed emporium. That is how I added some stunning French bean plants and precious tomatillos to my seedling tray. I made a deal to trade "extra" seedlings for kale and leaf lettuce plants, but then my plotting of the garden plot stalled.

Luckily, I had a brainwave and went online. I discovered that others have had success with harvesting seeds directly from purchased-for-consumption vegetables, like squash and tomatoes. The online gardening gurus note this only works with organics, as companies such as Monsanto have apparently altered the seeds in regular tomatoes so as to prevent re-seeding. This should be yet another reason to avoid any seeds except organic.

I had on hand a batch of organic plum tomatoes. Slavishly following the website directions, I scraped the seedy tomato "jelly" onto toilet paper as directed, dried them in the sun for a couple of days, and then planted then directly, TP and all, into my seedling pots. It worked! Those sprouts came up, thrived and grew side-by-side with my leftover-from-the-year-before San Marzano seeds. I couldn't tell the difference. The downside is that I can never replicate those, because even organic tomatoes are not sold in the supermarket by varietal name. I have no idea what I grew. But they tasted rich and had just the right consistency for freezer sauce (my favourite method of preserving toms). Silly me; I had intended to use the last one as a seed factory for this year, but forgot and ate it!

Emboldened, I experimented with winter squash, using the same technique minus the toilet paper. Again, I don't have any real idea what varietal it was, just your average butternut squash. This time the seeds did not grow true to the original plant, which may possibly have been Californian. My squash were tiny, whereas the mother plant had been a bruiser. This is the natural effect of a different climate, I suspect, and brings home to me the wisdom of the brilliant food writer Ruth Reichl, former editor of the sadly departed *Gourmet Magazine*: "For most of human history, farmers raised regional plants adapted to the local soil and climate. The idea that we can all grow anything, anywhere, is a completely modern notion – and one that makes very little sense. Organic gardeners are beginning to understand that the sensible course is to plant seeds bred to thrive where they are planted."

Notwithstanding Ms. Reichl's undoubted wisdom, I had beginner's luck with my unknown-source potato crop from rescues from the compost bin. Those organic Russets were happily growing shoots in the root veggie corner of my pantry. I just treated them like nursery-purchased seed potatoes. I cut each one into sprouting segments, preserving a minimum of one "eye" per spot in the prepared potato bed. A week later, up they came, the obliging little darlings! Thus inspired, I went out and bought a couple of organic baking potatoes, ate one, and deliberately ignored the other in its cool dark place until it, too, sprouted. Same technique and the same thing occurred. Lots of free potatoes! I love it when that happens.

Every garden bed needs soil amendments and my traditional go-to's are all totally natural. I favour a pre-planting mixture of seaweed (extra for the asparagus bed) and compost or compost tea (just add water). I get the seaweed from the beach down the road and I am not alone in my harvesting in the fall. I lay scads of it out on the drive-way, wait until it rains, which naturally de-brines it, and then spread it on the empty raised beds. I have a bin out back that gets fed constantly with everything compostable, except bones and fats. But the thing that makes me feel most like a real farmer is a big steamy batch of manure. Thanks to my husband and courtesy of a local organic horse, sheep, and cow farm, my Mother's Day gift was in the bag. My sweetie even put a bow on it!

There are a million ways to be a greener gardener and I urge you to check out the masses of good books and websites devoted to the cause. I even listen online to a great gardening show on BBC4 radio from the UK that provides me with all kinds of information (like peat is an endangered species, so don't use peat moss) and that teaches me environmentally sustainable tricks (like newspaper plant pots).

Despite the fact that I hadn't really budgeted for it, it was a grand YBN for the garden. I tried new things and relished the old reliables. I just love growing my own, and everybody loves eating them!

■ Chapter 6

Leftovers

ONCE UPON A TIME, IT WAS CONSIDERED GOOD ETIQUETTE TO REFRAIN FROM TWO CONTROVERSIAL TOPICS IF YOU WANTED TO HOST THE PERFECT PARTY: RELIGION AND POLITICS. These days, you just might have to avoid food as a subject for discussion. If your guests number more than 30, you will for sure have a vegetarian present, according to recent statistics. And a certain percentage of those will be vegans, who avoid all animal products, including dairy and eggs. (And cheese, no cheese! I couldn't do it!)

There may come a time when I give up meat, but that day isn't here yet. I am my father's child. He and I have spent hours in meat markets and with fishmongers from Kitchener, Ontario to Salmon Arm, British Columbia; from Albufiera, Portugal to Norwich, England, asking local butchers, *salumier* (deli), and sausage-makers detailed questions about their wares. I love good meat. My dad and I can talk about a roast beef dinner before, during, and after the event. I am mad about seafood. And now, I have learned to love meat that has been loved when it was on the hoof and treated as such animals should be treated, humanely. I routinely check an app that tells me the sustainability of the fish that tempts me.

You may be wondering how I justify sheltering a discussion of meat and the like in a section called "Vegetable." I will answer you simply: in our lives, these sources of protein are presented next to the other edibles on our plates. As such I have grouped them together as things we eat or drink, in this handy section. I beg the forgiveness of vegetarians in advance for the abuse of the vocabulary!

Having said all this, I now eat far less meat than I used to, and I treat animal-based proteins as a "condiment." This is Dan

Barber's marvellously argued approach in his book *The Third Plate*.

To give you an example: imagine a gorgeous meal set before you – an amazing Caesar salad with romaine from the garden, a single egg fresh from a local market and binding freshly squeezed lemon (so much nicer than vinegar); gorgeous, aged *parmigiana* cheese; and a generous number of garlicky buttery croutons made from a homemade whole-wheat French stick. Perched on top are beautifully grilled slices of a tiny beef striploin. This is a meal my husband and I love to make, and we split the beef striploin between us.

At four ounces in total, it represents one-quarter the amount of meat we would previously have consumed when we made steak and a salad. But I don't miss the *quantity* a bit, knowing that the *quality* is exactly what I demand of meat these days.

Despite what you might think, it wasn't difficult to switch to more ethical and sustainable sources of protein. The list of meat and poultry purveyors with a conscience grows daily. Even large supermarket chains are starting to get into the game. Locally, our beloved Getaway Farms (a butcher shop that sources beef from their own farm, and eco-friendly pork, lamb, and poultry from others of their ilk) is a standard-bearer for how to do it right. They have a farm-to-table approach and truly grow their own. And if you are thinking that is the privilege of living in or near a city, let me reassure you that I found a source of sustainably raised grass-fed beef while living in Curling, Newfoundland. It just doesn't get much smaller or more remote than that.

■ You are what your food eats

There are two primary reasons you should really pay attention to the meat products you consume. The first comes down to the axiom *you are what your food eats*.

The first reason to be knowledgeable about the meat you eat is so that you can ensure that you and your children are not consuming antibiotics and hormone-(steroid) growth supplements with every bite of chicken breast or roast beef. An incredible 80% of antibiotics sold in North America are for consumption by factory-farmed animals. And if you think you are steroid-free just because you don't take anything that sleazy muscled guy at the gym is peddling, think again. There is no way to avoid these additives unless you seek out sources that do not drug their animals so that they grow faster and can survive crowded and unsanitary conditions. Mercifully, this attitude is catching on. There is a product line at a large supermarket chain proudly marked "free from." I also hear a TV commercial from a fast-food chain that boasts its beef is free of antibiotics and preservatives and "added" hormones (not sure about that last bit, but it's a start!)

To begin, ask about meat that is "grass-fed" or "pastured." Here I am deeply indebted to an article by Bill Kiernan, "Grass Fed vs. Corn Fed: You Are What Your Food Eats," which is as concise and persuasive a summary of this complex issue as you could want. You can find it at the website of Global AgInvesting, where Kiernan was (July 2012) GAI's Director of Research.

"Cows are ruminants, superbly adapted to convert grass into meat or milk," states Kiernan in his opening statement. "Research is proving that the health concerns long associated with eating beef result not from eating beef, but rather from eating corn-fed beef." He goes on to describe how cattle were never designed by nature to eat corn. In fact, feeding cows corn creates acid levels in the stomach of the beast that lead to health conditions requiring the intervention of antibiotics, which in turn create a great environment for E. coli. And that disease is definitely not something you want to give someone you love.

So why, you ask, do ranchers feed corn to beef cattle? Because the cattle fatten up far faster than cows that eat grass. And faster-growing cows make for a more profitable herd. Commercial beef farmers have been feeding corn to cows in increasing amounts with larger and larger concentrations of antibiotics since World War II.

In modern beef production (the word "farming" doesn't really apply to industrial agri-businesses this massive), the calf is pastured for the first few months then brought into an intensive food lot, where the animal's diet becomes largely corn: corn augmented by antibiotics, growth hormones, and protein supplements (steroids). While once it took up to five years for a beef cow to be readied for slaughter, that time has been lowered to approximately 14 months. I am sure you are seeing the profit motive grow here?

But the additives in the corn do something much more sinister than reduce the time to slaughter. According to Kiernan, "Feeding cattle on corn fundamentally changes the meat they produce, greatly increasing levels of unhealthy Omega-6 fatty acids and decreasing levels of healthy Omega-3 fatty acids. This change greatly impacts the healthiness of meat for human consumption."

Cows raised on grass have high recorded levels of conjugated linoleic acid (CLA). CLA is the healthy acid that is credited with preventing heart disease, diabetes, and that plays a role in bodyweight management. CLA is also a natural anti-carcinogen. Its measureable levels in the systems of corn-fed beef drop dramatically and after six months on the corn-intensive, food-lot diet it has vanished from the cow's body.

So let's connect the dots. Beef producers changed the diet of cattle from grass to corn to shorten the time it takes to raise a cow to slaughter, from five years to 14 months. In the process, this increased the level of unhealthy Omega 6 fatty acids in the meat, decreased the level of healthy Omega-3 acids, and obliterated the presence of the anti-carcinogen, diabetes- and heart-disease-preventing CLA. Although certainly not the only cause, it seems clear there is a connection between these practices and the rampant increase in diabetes, heart disease, and weight gain we see today.

You need only look around at all the chubby children to get the weight management issue. Compare a class photo from the 1950s with one from a Fourth-Grade classroom today if you really want to shock yourself. Diabetes? Look at the information from the societies that represent that disease. And as for cancer, look around the circle of your family and friends.

I recently read a marvellous book: *Memoir of a Cape Breton Doctor*. It is the story of Dr. C Lamont MacMillan, a family physician who practised from 1928 to 1965 in the remote areas of Nova Scotia. The tale is remarkable for its portrait of seemingly insurmountable transportation difficulties and the derring-do of a wise and courageous man, backed by his trusty horse and armed with a sense of humour outstripped only by his humility. He speaks of death and suffering, yes, of childbirth mortality and dreadful accidents from tractor falls and drowning. But he does not encounter cancer, or at least it is an infrequent meeting. Pneumonia and tuberculosis and various septic ailments, yes – but not cancer.

There may be other factors contributing to the increase in heart disease, diabetes and cancer, but this was a wake-up call to me. I spent a great deal of time looking at the simple logic of the argument against artificially hurried-to-slaughter cattle and made up my mind about future consumption of beef. The sad tale was persuasive enough to convert me entirely to meats that are not corn-fed, and chicken that is not factory-farmed, and lamb from sheep that are allowed to graze on grass, and pork that I can see eating something other than corn. It also converted me to eating *way* less of any of it! Enough said.

■ Avoid animal cruelty

The second reason to pay attention to the meat products you consume is so that you can avoid meat sources that employ practices that are cruel to the animals involved.

The better you know your source, the more you can be reassured that animals did not suffer unduly so that *you* can tuck into a good meal. This means that those who raised the cattle or the chickens or the sheep took all possible precautions to minimize animal suffering during growth, and that they were killed humanely in a responsible slaughterhouse. Yes, you can and *should* ask: a good butcher will know the answer to where that roast came from because he or she should care. Frankly, it is imperative to me now to know that my purchase is not the root-cause of the torture of another living creature.

Humane farms is a term to seek. Current owners of farms who care deeply about decency in animal husbandry are putting pressure on Canadian government agencies that have the responsibility to oversee meat production, so that this terminology becomes better understood. This is true also of American farmers and the USDA, which is useful as so much of our meat and poultry comes from our southern neighbours. Join the pressure to uphold and increase existing standards by seeking out humanely raised animal protein. Become an informed meat-eater. To better understand this position, check an excellent web article at Vegan.com entitled "Evaluating Whole Foods Market's Animal Welfare Rating System." But this is not a trend limited only to that one supermarket chain. Watch for a growing number of grocery stores who are getting wise to the marketing usefulness of promoting decency to animals for human consumption. I commend both Sobeys and the President's Choice (Loblaws) chains for offering more product lines from humane farms every year.

■ A bargain at twice the price

The hard truths associated with the industrial-scale meat production industry can make it more difficult to take advantage of the "bargains" on meat and poultry with a clear conscience.

And another hard truth is that there are no "bargains" price-wise, when it comes to humanely raised and grass-fed meat products. They are simply more costly and the difference is much greater than that for fruits and vegetables that are "cleaner" (generally 25% to 50% more at my supermarket). You can expect to pay as much as double the price for grass-fed beef. That's because of the corn-fed process, among other factors. Remember: 14 months versus four to five years of growth?

But Ann Hodgman, author of the wonderful and witty *Beat This!* and *Beat That! Cookbook* series raises a good question: "Does the fact that most people can't afford to buy humanely raised meat mean that those of us who can shouldn't?"

I couldn't afford to eat humanely raised and grass-fed meat if we consumed it the way we did as newlyweds, when our weekly list started with the following: beef x 3 meals, pork x 1 meal, chicken x 2 meals, and something else. We don't eat that way anymore. As an example, let me take you through what we did with an appropriately sourced, humanely raised ham that we served initially for a family feast and enjoyed well beyond. The price was $8 per pound, which is probably double what you might expect to pay for a bone-in-shoulder cut. Our ham was six pounds, or $48, and would have been beyond our budget had we not made that beast fulfill its destiny. This is what we did with it.

■ glazed ham (with scalloped potatoes, carrots, etc.) – 5 servings
■ hot ham leftovers – 2 servings
■ ham sandwiches – 8 servings
■ ham-and-noodle casserole – 4 servings
■ ham and lentil bake – 2 servings
■ ham and root veggies au gratin – 4 servings
■ navy bean soup (with ham bone) – 12 servings

So that brought a $48 purchase down into the sane world where real people eat at $1.30 per serving. And *that* we can afford. In fact, we can't afford to do otherwise, for the sake of our planet and our health.

■ A finny afterword

Living, as we do, right on the ocean, we are spoiled for choice when it comes to fresh fish. We stick to sustainable species of ocean or freshwater fish and shellfish, as locally caught as possible. There are detailed treatises on the issue of farm fisheries. There may be well-managed ones that avoid heavy doses of antibiotics and that do not permit their hatchlings to escape to maraud the native fledgling fish stock. I don't know them. We don't eat fish from them. If I see salmon on a menu, I ask where it comes from. If the waiter doesn't know or care, I order something else. There is an app called Seafood Watch for checking which species are okay to eat, and which are endangered. You wouldn't eat tiger meat, would you? How can you possibly justify chowing down on Atlantic bluefin (*thunnus thynnus*) tuna just to satisfy a craving for sushi?

■ Finally, a toast!

I did promise prose on potables. Let's start with the obvious: water. We are on a drilled-well system. That's good, especially as we live in a part of Nova Scotia where the well bed is free of the nasty things that many wells are plagued with: E. coli, arsenic (from long-ago mining processes), and drought. We get our well checked regularly. I drink that tap-water all the time, cook with it, and boil endless cups of it for tea. My husband does not. I respect his wishes and he takes responsibility for our supply of giant bottles for the cooler in our kitchen. They are made from the "good" (non-leaching) plastic. We have had them for some time now and continue to carefully sanitize and reuse them.

Individual plastic water bottles are a different matter entirely. I, along with millions of other North Americans, abhor these parasitic one-use bottles and refuse them entry to our home or our car. Yet estimates put the annual number dumped into the ocean at over 60 billion. They kill fish and mammals. They pollute as they break down into smaller and smaller pieces. (The plastic itself never breaks down or disintegrates at the molecular level.) The giant producer-manufacturers like Nestle, Pepsico, and Perrier have been filling them from sources they are coy about, including California, where drought is a huge problem. There is just no excuse for this. If you make only one lifestyle change, this would be the one to make: stop purchasing and consuming single-use plastic bottles; they clutter our beaches, drain our waterways, and clog our landfills.

You already know that we drink milk and tea. And coffee. There are organic and sustainable sources for all of the above and we already talked about milk. Ask your tea seller, your barista, or read the labels and check out the details on your favourite bevvy. I freely confess to a seasonal craving for a certain holiday beverage from Starbucks, which I satisfy once a year without asking too many questions. On the other hand, I am very picky about my daily cappuccino and know its pedigree exactly. It is a matter of degree, isn't it?

And finally, the fun part! My grandmother was largely an abstainer, but would "take a drink" at holidays – a single, small glass of Scotch whiskey. My grandfather told a story of remaining at home by the fireside on Castlefield Avenue in Toronto, sipping good malt whiskey with a visiting Wesley McClung, while "the wives" (Nellie McClung and my grandmother) attended a meeting of the Women's Christian Temperance Union. My father and uncle both worked for breweries all their lives. My father-in-law worked for the Liquor Control Board of Ontario. So it would be hypocritical in the extreme and a big fat lie if I said I do not enjoy a bit of the grape and the grain myself.

My tipple depends on the season, the food, and the mood. "Drinking responsibly" does not, for me, mean avoiding getting behind the wheel after I've had a drink. It *does* increasingly entail checking on the source of what I put in my mouth, in a recipe, and on the table for guests.

I have familiarized myself with the terms *organic* and *biodynamic* and *sustainable* as they apply to wine and other forms of alcoholic drinks. Organic in this context means pretty much what we understood from our tour of produce. You can seek out a label that says "made with organically-grown grapes" and be reasonably assured that it does not contain pesticides, herbicides, and fungicides. However, if sulphites are an issue, you should look for the label "certified organic wines." The first label, even certified by a third-party endorsement, does not ensure total lack of sulphites, as the wine may have been processed in a facility that also processed wines that *did* contain that substance, which is troublesome for asthmatics. The terms "biodynamic" and "sustainable," on the other hand, suffer from definition-shift when it comes to wine, and their meanings are quite murky, in my opinion.

However, I am not totally persuaded that these crops – the barley, the hops, the grapes, and the grains – *are* as plagued by the horrors of residual pesticides, fungicides, and herbicides as other edibles. The online literature is not terribly helpful on this score. There is some talk of fluoride caused by a pesticide used on Californian grapes. There are certainly folks that don't like the big vintners in Australia, for example, but they are lean on facts and high on claims of wine that felt "heavy in the back of the throat."

On the other side of the argument, some claim that greater personal attention to the vines and the hops from individual growers implies less dependence on growth additives, and that we should look to countries and sources of wine that are collected from ancient vines, wine sourced from Italy and France. But I am pretty certain I saw giant swathes of vineyards in those countries, too.

There are sources that claim that the processing of alcoholic beverages destroys the damage done by the chemical agents used in growing. But if that were the case, surely the cooking to which I subject, say spinach, one of the Dirty Dozen, would solve the residue problems of that vegetable. No one is claiming that cooking eliminates the toxins left on produce. So perhaps these are all well-paid apologists for the non-organic alcohol industry I have been reading? I can't tell. There are voices, for example, that recommend only organic sources for grapes as the way to go. Quite a number of these appear to be linked to organic vintners. It all remains a bit of a mystery.

Here is a good time to reveal why I am not as vigilant about the toxic qualities that may plague alcoholic beverages as I am about fruits, veggies, meat, and fish. I do not serve alcoholic beverages to children. A great deal of my vigour about keeping food free of toxic chemicals is aimed at keeping small bodies as untainted as possible. Now, I am not saying that everyone over 18 is fair game for suicide-by-pesticide at my table, but we can at least make our own choices; I can relax my hypervigilance. Personally, while I enjoy a glass of wine, I mean that *literally*.

For very light drinkers, how much caution to exercise may strictly be a matter of personal preference, as there are probably few real health risks. Anyway, that's my bias disclosed for the record. Back to the booze.

Issues of how source materials for alcoholic beverages are grown are not limited to wine. There are whiskey distilleries that use only organically-tended barley. I have seen a number of organic vodkas and a rum offering. There are undoubtedly more varieties coming. And there are an increasing number of organic brews for the beer lover. Though I have tried and like several organic and biodynamic wines and a beer or two that we find locally, I can't vouch for the taste of your favourite beverage versus traditional tipples, distillations, and brews.

But all this talk makes me thirsty and it does inspire in me "a great notion" (with apologies to Ken Kesey). My father was in market research with a major Canadian brewery for much of his working life. Those pioneers of marketing invented the "taste-test." In our house growing up, there was always a taste test underway – not, I hasten to add, a beer taste test.

Both my parents were very moderate drinkers, as is the habit of many I have known who work with alcohol on a regular basis and view first-hand the dark side of abuse. No, our tests were votes for the comparative deliciousness of homemade versus boxed chocolate pudding. Or which tastes better, a rare versus well-done outside cut of roast beef? Or could my sister and I tell the difference between cheddar from that farmer's market versus the stuff in the big yellow box with the red letters? (We could and did; we remain cheese snobs and proud of it.)

So here is my idea. Let's have a national taste-off! Organics versus non-organics of your favourite beverage! Who's with me? Chill the white, put the beer on ice, get out the good glasses and take tiny little sips. Doesn't that sound like a wonderful game for a summer afternoon or evening by the fire?

■ Part III

Mineral

(about getting there, staying warm,
and keeping it light)

■ Chapter 7

Conserving Energy

THIS AREA CAUSED ME GREATER CHALLENGE THAN ANY OTHER DURING MY YBN. In my mind, buying nothing beyond those items that were pre-budgeted truly meant not putting my hand in my pocket, signature to cheque, or pulling out that credit card for anything that was not stated in the rules I committed to in advance.

Turns out Robbie Burns was correct: "the best-laid schemes o' mice an' men gang aft agley ..." The plans for this country-used-to-be-city mouse went astray badly in the second week. And it didn't get better after that. Stuff happens, like the man said. There are transportation emergencies, the bread machine walks off the job, you forget your pledge and find yourself with a forbidden object in your hand, or there is a book you just *must have* to share with someone you love.

■ Getting from A to B without compromising O (the Ozone level)

The rules that I put in place for myself said that as far as getting around is concerned, transportation was to be limited to essentials: utilizing public buses in town or in the country (we lived in both that year), and / or a family car that was making the trip anyway. I have the advantage of many of you in that I have had lots of practice getting around without refilling the gas tank of my car. I don't have a car. Never did. I don't have a driver's licence, because I never learned to drive. Yes, that's me: one of the few people you have ever met that don't and never did drive. It is difficult to get an accurate statistic on exactly how many people in North America are drivers, but some experts suggest that even if they have given up their licences, approximately 96% of all citizens of eligible driving age do have the capability of driving and have been a registered driver at some point. Some of them probably shouldn't drive, but that's not the point of this story. I know I am a minority and a shrinking one at that.

I never listed *not driving* as a life goal, though it turned to be a strategy that served me very well. I wasn't all that keen on learning to drive. I had my trusty CCM bike (one-speed, pedal brakes). I was and am a good walker. As a teenager in St. John's, Newfoundland, I truly loved dreaming for hours as I walked those hilly, picturesque streets. And I like buses. People on buses talk to each other, especially those in small towns. Everywhere I have ever lived, except in this small coastal town in the Maritimes, buses have been part of my transportation life. Along with a concerned group of age-friendly and environmentally savvy activists, I hope to add buses to this town's roads for tomorrow's citizenry.

I did *try* to learn to drive, but this effort at age 17 ended in a small-but-compromising failure on my fifth attempt behind the wheel. That's a story for another day, but suffice it to say I just never got around to trying again. I have a brilliant legal-eagle cousin in England, one the brightest people I have ever known; he had three or four car accidents before the age of 21, not attributed to the usual youth-related causes of over-confidence or alcohol. For Cousin, it was either preoccupation or overthinking that caused him to end up against a wall, or get rear-ended due to an inability to commit to a turn. He gave up his licence and lives a normal and successful non-driving life, too. Genetic? Both my parents were excellent drivers, going life-long without incident or accident. My sister is a competent and calm driver, too, as is our daughter. Me? Sometimes even today I dream I am forced by circumstances to steer a car. I wake up panicky, palms sweating.

When I was in my 20s, friends would preach to me about the deprivations of a life without a car. I ignored them and truly have never felt the lack. Not driving has worked for me in so many ways. My husband and I are very close, and part of that is the time we spend together in the car. He is my rock in life and my faithful charioteer, never once in all these years raising the expectation that I should take the wheel and thereby take the stress off him. In fact, he agrees that I don't have the kind of brain that makes for good driving. We have had many of the truly significant conversations of our lives sitting side by side in the car. When our daughter was a teen, if Daddy drove her somewhere, Mum went along for the ride. We always encouraged her to offer friends a lift home; kids talk in the back of a car, especially if there are two adults in the front amusing one another, seemingly ignoring them. You can learn a lot about young people by listening to their casual chatter.

In the workplace, not being a driver was my secret strategic management tool. If there was an outside meeting, someone would offer to drive me. Nothing permits in-depth "getting to know you" sessions like the enforced intimacy of a car stuck in downtown traffic. I *really* knew our staff and my colleagues back in the publishing world, in ways that other managers never achieved. It is my experience that people reveal themselves behind the wheel of a car. I would go so far as to say that 90% of my current pastoral skills were gained by truly listening to a driver unburden, as only those who don't have to make eye contact will do.

Okay: I don't want to get creepy about this. I am guessing that round about now everyone who ever gave me a lift is wondering what the h— they might have unwittingly revealed. So moving right along, let me tell you what happened during week two of my YBN.

Very early in the year, I was committed to a church-related speaking engagement that required a pre-meeting. As it was my vow to stick to "shared" travel (buses or cars with multiple passengers), I was pleased when my daughter offered me a lift as she headed to work. We had plenty of time to travel eight miles, even in city traffic.

The first mile, we heard an ominous sound but studiously ignored it, raising the decibel level of our mom-daughter chatter. The second mile, we reassured each other that the noise was "probably the muffler," something that to our non-mechanical minds could safely be ignored for months. Mile three, the car listed to one side and made frightening grinding noises. We pulled over and gazed at what was clearly a totally flat tire; we had been riding on the rim. My daughter phoned for a tow and let her office know that she was going to be late.

I was five miles and 10 minutes from that meeting. No time for the bus, even if I knew which to catch in an unknown section of town. Do I phone and announce to the assembled roomful of good church volunteers that I have to reschedule? Or do I put common sense and courtesy to others ahead of my YBN rule of "no taxis"?

Sitting in the back of that inevitable cab I came to the sobering realization that this year was going to be harder than I thought. And it was. We will leave the other frustrations for a little further on, because I want to explore the issue of travelling light, by which I do not mean one suitcase, but rather without besmirching the environment more than we must.

■ Planes, trains, and automobiles ... and buses

You are not going to get a lecture from me on how to curb your car enthusiasm. Yes, I think it is sad that what was once ownership of a family car has morphed into automatic entitlement to a personal automobile. Yes, I am aware that the gas consumption and carbon emission from all those added vehicles on the road is a huge determinant in global warming. Yes, I really believe in car-sharing options and I know a number of families that *can* and *do* make that work. But overall, would you listen to me on this anymore than an alcoholic would welcome a sermon from a lifelong teetotaller? I don't think so.

So what I will tell you instead is what a wonderful year I had in buses and driving with others and walking everywhere I went. Only one time other than the occasion I just shared was I forced into a taxi. Ironically, that was because I had to be at a TV studio to do an interview about my YBN blog – husband away on business and the hour was too early for buses (interview time: 7

a.m., minus an hour-and-a half for makeup and "Green Room," which, in reality, was a stool in the hall chatting with a cameraperson on break. This stuff is *so* not glamourous.) Yikes, call a cab!

For the remainder of my city needs, the bus service in our town served quite well. I had come to rely on subways and bus service back in my other career in Toronto. I like buses, sitting up and looking around, enjoying the view, being in from the cold or out of the heat, reading my book or prepping for a meeting. And, yes, talking to that person beside me. Not intrusively, I trust, but if you say to the woman in the red coat, the one not lost to the printed page or her iPod, "that colour suits you," and she smiles, you are away to the conversational races. The smallest remark has sparked really interesting conversations on long bus rides. I cannot tell you how often a person has confided that they were really glad I said hello. There is so much loneliness in the world.

During my YBN, I also had the care and entertainment of a young gentleman to consider. My (then) two-year-old grandson loved everything about going on the bus. He was going through a love-affair-with-vehicles phase. Just waiting at the bus stop and seeing that giant grille coming down the hill towards us was exciting. There was a friendly driver and people on the bus who took an interest in his enthusiasm for what was on view outside the window: "Nana Lee! Look!! A crane!!!" What's more, that bus took us to fascinating places, like the library, the Natural History Museum, and the grocery store where the cashier gave out tiny boxes of raisins. If you want to renew your zest for life, borrow a little pal and take a bus ride.

Major solo bus trips —such as from Boston, Massachusetts, to Augusta, Maine; or from Toronto to Peterborough, Ontario; reap rewards, too. I have sat, at different times, beside a man who was en route to a reunion with his adult son after years of separation; a woman who rescued, of all things, parrots; and, most movingly, a young girl heading home from the big, bad city to her family at Christmas, pregnant and afraid. I turned this latter incident into a story for *The United Church Observer,* and it gets asked for again and again at congregations where I preach. I have also twice been witness to police interventions on bus platforms. I know that bus travel is considered beyond the pale by many people. Bus stations may be the last corner of any city to get gentrified. But I still feel stubbornly loyal to my fellow Greyhound travellers. If more of us took the bus, there would be better service, more congenial depots, less automobile traffic, and lower rates of air pollution. There I've said it.

My love affair with trains is rooted in one of few memories I have of my paternal grandfather. In my mind's eye, I am four years of age and walking down a street in Birmingham, England, clutching Gwa's hand. ("Gwa" is the traditional name for grandfathers in my dad's family, honouring a mangling of "Grampa" from long ago.) I am all dressed up as we are going to the place where Gwa, now retired, has a work connection. Now that I am a grandparent myself, I realize that it was *me* that was being shown off. I had been given a train set for Christmas. All I cared about was being accorded the chance to see a *real* example of those beautiful, scary iron beasts up close. We were headed for a behind-the-scenes-tour of the train yards. That day remains with me still: the smell, the sounds, the vibrations, the whoosh of air as the monstrous passenger trains of Great Britain in the 1950s entered and exited the busy station yard. Through the years, I have spent many hours exploring train stations, and catching trains, too. I have travelled in all classes and have slept in Wagonlit (the sleeper cars of European trains: the backdrop for many a racy moment in the memories of "hippies" of the '60s and '70s). Terminals are places of romance and trains things of massive steel magnificence to me still. To my mind, the most evocative Canadian tune remains not our actual national anthem, but Gordon Lightfoot's *Canadian Railroad Trilogy.*

Taking off my rose-coloured glasses, there are also some comforting carbon-emission statistical reasons for taking a train versus, for example, a plane. For the run from Toronto to Montreal, the kilograms per passenger seat of carbon spewed into the air if you travel on Via Rail is less than a fifth of what it is if you fly Air Canada, for example. Not even a contest. And in Europe, where train technology is way ahead of North American (where rail progress has stalled completely) the figures in favour of the train versus flight are staggering. You can save 91% of the carbon vapours that would be expended on a flight from London to Paris by taking the Eurostar train instead.

Living in Europe for a time really spoiled me for ground travel. The bus and train systems for getting from city to city and from tiny village to town are so far ahead of our options that our complacency here in North America seems shocking to me. Italians and Germans simply recognize the work-agenda wisdom of the downtown Milan to Berlin train option, and get on board. I routinely rode the bus for an hour from our town in the Abruzzo, into Rome, with an array of suited and coifed businesspersons. It is a rare executive indeed on our continent that even *considers* the bus or train versus plane for city hops.

We can change this relatively recent pattern of destructive behaviour. The EU has done so, deliberately adopting train-friendly legislation and is the better for it. Planes are the fastest growing contributor to carbon emissions and there are more of them in the skies every year due to our increasing demand. We must re-examine our travel options and choices in light of the pressures of climate change and other damage to the environment.

Just as with our toothpaste (avoid micro-beads!) and our face creams (ban the parabens!), we have buying power if only we choose to exercise it. If we demand it, they will make it happen – better, safer, faster, and then it will get cheaper, too. Join a movement to bring back train travel and support politicians who advocate for maintenance of our rail lines and increases in train-travel options. Support Maritime Bus (or NeOn or your local equivalent bus line). Ride the Greyhound Line and chat to your fellow passengers. Good for the soul, it is! And definitely better for the earth.

Having said all that, there are times when the alternative

simply does not exist. I encountered just such a situation during my YBN, which brought home to me again the unexpected turns of life, the graciousness of both friends and strangers, and the necessity of compromise.

■ Flying in the face of all good intentions

My friend and I shared a name and enthusiasm for the open road. Lee knew she was dying and made appropriate travel plans for that journey, too. What she didn't foresee was the outpouring of love and friendship that accompanied her end. In her final weeks, others sent vast bouquets, organized deliveries of smoked meat from Montreal, and box upon box of candy from places she had visited. From Nice to New Zealand, her sweet tooth was legendary. This childless, modest, single 70-year-old was overwhelmed with tributes. And Lee asked me for something, too. From 1,000 miles away, she requested that I preside over her Celebration of Life service. I gave that as my gift, unhesitatingly. Even though we would not be able to plan the timing, as death rarely gives appropriate notice for travel options other than flying, I could not and would not have done otherwise.

Lee's budget had always been tight. She was a thrifty and gutsy traveller. Just before her final illness, she spent six weeks in South America, patronizing only local buses, hostels, and street-food vendors. When she travelled, she departed alone, but she rarely remained so. She made friends via the travel website forum where we first "met." Those relationships crossed barriers of language and geography, as people travelled to meet her in person. Her touring bravado sprang from her absolute faith in the kinship of humanity. This high-school dropout, driver-for-a-car-dealership, self-deprecating woman, was not disappointed, counting among her circle of friends architects, entrepreneurs, artists, professors, poets, and doctors. She once spent an afternoon drinking iced tea with Phil of the Everley Brothers.

I had to be there for her, and for all her extended circle. But there were hurdles in this race. Beyond the flight itself, getting to the memorial service in a town far from the one where the plane landed required throwing myself on the mercy of others to avoid breaking further YBN rules. I overnighted with a girl-friend in exchange for a homemade meal on her return from work. I cajoled a colleague, David Wilson, editor-publisher of *The United Church Observer* into helping me out, too, which he, as ever, very graciously did. The deal was this: he required a business meeting with me; I coerced him into driving me 80 kilometres to the service (and buying me a coffee too!).

There were over 200 present at Lee's Celebration of Life, and more than 600 written and emailed tributes from around the world. The food was good and the tears and laughter flowed. When those who had remembered Lee that day started to slip away from the feast, I approached a couple I knew slightly and asked outright for a ride back to the city where I would catch my plane home. The confessional intimacy of that car, in the pour-ing rain, post-funeral, transformed acquaintanceship into the beginnings of deep friendship – the ultimate recycling act!

When it comes to environmental impact, planes are the worst way to go, with individual cars next, and buses and trains the least problematical. None of this is definitive and all statistics vary based on how many passengers are involved and the kind of fuel used. But basically, that's the order if you have the luxury of time and money in making your decision.

Knowing all this, but having no way to justify a month-long leave from work to arrange the logistics of bus and train travel to get to my dad, who lives in British Columbia, for one of my twice-yearly visits, I discussed in advance with my Okanagan-based sister my YBN reasons for leaving it all until the New Year. We stuck with that plan, which was fine with my dad and step-mum, keen emailers who love the pics we send with our mes-sages every few days. That, along with the Sunday phone call, sufficed... until my dad, 92, did something he had never done before and got sick. In fact, he experienced what he described as "a heart event." My sister, who works in a geriatric facility nearby, took off the month of June to help Dad make some lifestyle adjustments so he and my amazing step-mum could continue in their home until the new condo in a more accessible area of the province was move-in ready.

I felt the need to be there, too: both duty and my heart called the shots on this one. I tried to make it as YBN-friendly as possible, from everything except the carbon point of view. Using points to get there meant I had to pay a price in sane scheduling – what should have been an 8-hour trip took 17 hours. My poor sister had to wait up past midnight to greet me at the airport. I had planned the treat of asparagus from my garden as a hostess gift, but I ended up ditching my spears and purchasing organic-market replacements for an unearthly price. Note to self: three-day-old limp, wilted greens do not say "Happy Father's Day!"

My fellow voracious-reader sister saved me from terminal boredom and more YBN sins. For the four-airport, 20-hour marathon home, she presented me with an early birthday gift: a chunky book that eased the pain of those airline seats. The bottom line ethically? I spent that special Sunday holding my Dad's hand, sharing his favourite dessert (fruit cocktail and ice cream), and watching soccer. We both silently acknowledged the future. And that day I was exactly where I was supposed to be.

Another vacation decision was also a compromise, but one that went the other way. Great pals and travelling companions enticed us to join them for two weeks in France, where they had booked roomy accommodation in Paris and the Dordogne, as a celebration of retirement and anniversary. All we needed to contribute was ourselves, transportation, and sous-chef skills. It was hard to say "no," but my supportive husband agreed that this was not the year. We joined them at home for a send-off party instead. A wonderful meal with contributions from others of our circle, then music provided by both guests and hosts: chords of piano, guitar, accordion, and autoharp consolidated the friendship.

I learned a lot during the decision-making sessions surrounding these plane trips, both the one I took and the one my husband and I passed on. Ours is uniquely blessed as the first generation that air travel has impacted so heavily. Once upon a time, emigrating meant never seeing your parents again. Now we have the unbelievable luxury of being able to get home within hours, to virtually anywhere in the world. It is very hard to justify not doing so if we are at all financially capable of making that trip every few years. But our environment pays the cost of every plane ride to see relations, to attend a business meeting, and to vacation in the sunny south. It is one of the toughest decisions we as a family make. As a result, I have few absolute lessons to offer in this area, as witnessed by my two air trips in a year I did not plan to fly at all.

But I did learn some other things. Whether it be your final days or you are simply committed to a difficult path, lean on others. There is a blessed benefit to admitting you cannot do it all by yourself.

■ "It's too dark in here to adjust the thermostat"

Let's stop fuelling around. What can we do to relieve the stress on our environment, without giving up domestic heat and light? It is well beyond the scope of this book to address the big question of what your primary source of home heating should be. So many of the articles and books I read seemed to address the needs of someone planning to build their own house from foundation to roof, but my research suggested that this is a situation that fewer than .5% of us will ever find ourselves in. That's a lot of ink expended preaching to a small group of lucky souls. More power to you if that is your situation, for you can control every element of the issue of what kind of heating will work best for you and the planet.

But most of us live in an environment dictated by decisions taken long ago. If you live in an apartment building, or rent a flat, you have no choice about how the building is heated. Should you own a condominium, you may have some influence, if you get on the board and the building is reviewing its fuel options during your term. If you own your home and have the finances for a renovation, you could replace the furnace, switching out oil for natural gas, natural gas for electricity, adding solar panels or, if you have enough useable property, you could opt for geothermal.

I have friends who live totally off the grid, utilizing a wood stove and wind turbine combination. They know themselves to be blessed. The planet and I both thank them. It is a huge commitment of time and personal energy: maintaining the turbines, managing the woodlot, cutting and replanting trees, and chopping and hauling wood. It is also a task they admit they will not be able to keep up for more than a decade as they approach their late-60s now.

For most of us, though, we are limited to minor adjustments of existing variables when it comes to being kind to the environment while staying warm in a cold land.

During my YBN, I committed us to heating only with wood. My husband was a little less than fulsome in his endorsement of this idea, but I loved it. We have a wood stove that heats our home and lights up my life. Gosh, I am nuts about that thing! In the event of a house fire, the stove would be the first inanimate object I'd grab.

I might even be a pyromaniac, as I love starting fires and gazing at them endlessly. Mercifully, I do not suffer from the lack of impulse control that would push my flirtation with fire over the edge. Uncontrolled spontaneity is not my problem. Indeed, my fires are well-planned.

I did not grow up around fires. We didn't have a working fireplace until I was in my teens and then it was chiefly for decoration. At Christmas, Dad would purchase a garishly labelled fake log from a gas station, wrestle with the flue, and light that sucker. The whole family would say nice things while choking on thick black smoke and feeling the warmth of a "clean" oil furnace escape up the chimney.

We also were not campers. In fact, I'd classify our family as *anti-campers*. The idea of my elegant mother hosting a fireside meal outside a tent gives me the giggles. Suffice it to say, lighting fires was not part of my past.

But now the heart of our home is a cast-iron, wood-burning stove, a green enamel and brass thing of beauty. It waits for autumn beside the stairs in the living/dining area. Well-set and all fired up, it heats our entire home for free! Being careful with a dime, I adore that part. With a few passes of our chainsaw, an afternoon with the wood-splitter and mandatory two-year aging period, we turn the windfall trees on our property into warmth each year to combat the bitterest winter blast.

There are areas in this country where wood burning is actively discouraged and in some cities it is a matter of debate, so read up on the pros and cons and check local municipal regulations before purchasing a wood stove. But out here, and from my perspective, it is eco-friendly and a good alternative to burning fossil fuel. And we can continue to grow trees – they are, after all, a renewable resource – if we remain good stewards. But managing a woodlot well requires research. Not all trees are created equal when it comes to their potential for burning cleanly. Our education was hard-won, as was my fire-setting prowess. Initially, I didn't get it. Then I met a chimney sweep, a much-revered community asset, who gravely instructed me in the art of layering: paper spills, twig kindling, stumpy small branches, then, artfully arched against the back of the furnace, two big logs. One match, adjust the draft, and whoosh! In winter, it just goes and goes.

We can also cook on our wood stove, which means when the electricity goes off, as it does frequently, our non-wood-stove neighbours can join us and find food. This past winter was ferocious and the power went down several times. I learned to keep the ingredients for simple casseroles on hand: wieners and beans and lentils and cheese do well on the cook-top of a wood stove. Like my neighbour Nellie, who taught me so much about life out here, I keep a kettle ready for tea or coffee as well. I have baked potatoes in the coals and we have opened the door long enough to toast marshmallows for a delighted grandchild, too.

And I gaze wonderingly into this practical marvel. I watch it ignite, holding my breath for that moment of conversion, when latent smoke turns to brilliant flame. I remain amazed by the predictability of the flame patterns, like living things, dancing in choreographed sequence. It is a thing of beauty.

My theory is that even though we have an oil-burning furnace at the ready, every litre of fossil fuel we *don't* burn is a boon for the environment. Certainly in our situation, this is a kindness we can do to the planet. You will have to judge your own situation and make your own plans to cut back your footprint.

Now, in the interests of full disclosure, the wood-heat-only stipulation only applied during the portion of the year we spent at our home in the country, not when we were house-sitting in the city. Then, like many people, we had to make do with an oil-burning furnace. There are things we can all do, of course, and you will know them as well as I do, but these are the ones that meant the most to us.

Turn down the thermostat of your oil burning, natural gas, or electric heat source. Put them on timers if your life is as predictable as ours is (up at 6 a.m., down by 10 p.m.). All these sources carry a carbon footprint that is going to be made smaller by your conservation. It is amazing how quickly your body adjusts. We keep the temperature at 67°F (19.5°C) during the day, and 60°F (15.5°C) at night. When I was a kid, the norms were 72°F (22.2°C) and 68°F (20°C). I would find that stifling now.

If you feel chilly, reach first for a sweater or cozy throw rug, before you put up the temperature. Ensure that you are not losing heat through windows or lack of insulation or other sources of avoidable loss. There are agencies and utility providers that offer energy audits of your home usage at little or no cost.

When it came to lighting, I learned a thing or two during my YBN. We had a supply of non-incandescent alternative bulbs that we hadn't quite got around to trying, as we tended to keep replacing our burnt-out bulbs with the old standby from Edison's day. Yes, we did know better, but we needed that kick to get us going. We resisted breaking my YBN rules, tested the store of long-resisted alternatives, and were enlightened!

To truly curb power usage, do the right thing and turn your

lights and appliances off at every opportunity. Personally, I have trained myself to flip the switch, but if you have folks in your home who don't, do think about timers for areas where lights get forgotten. Think also of the security aspect of having lights on timers when you are away from home, if your area is a target for theft. Just ensure your timer lets you set the security light to come on at random intervals. There is nothing that is such a dead giveaway to a would-be burglar as 8 a.m. on and 10 p.m. off, in an ever-repeating cycle. (This was a tip shared by one of the helpers in the soup kitchen where I volunteered in a downtown urban area. *He* learned it in prison.)

Beyond simply turning off your lights, we can, of course, switch to more energy-efficient bulbs. Canada began phasing out incandescent light bulbs in 2014, when the federal government prohibited the manufacture and importation into Canada of all 75w and 100w incandescent bulbs. The phase out continued in 2015, with the extension of the ban to 40w and 60w bulbs. These bulbs can still be sold, and you can still purchase them, but only while stockpiles last, and that won't be forever.

Some people aren't fond of the most common replacements, CFLs (compact fluorescent lights), because they're not as good in situations where one needs directed light, but in these situations halogens work very well. The other option is LED lights, and fortunately, though still comparatively expensive now, the price will continue to fall as demand increases. They use 90% less power and last up to 25 times longer than incandescents, so the benefits, in terms of our energy consumption and the resultant impacts on the environment, are significant.

Next: unplug appliances when not in use. There really isn't much purpose in keeping your laptop going all night, or your charging dock plugged in with nothing in it. If you are really committed, unplug everything that you possibly can that has a glowing element. The fridge has to stay on and it is really difficult to unplug a regular stove. But the microwave, coffee maker, laptop, and iPod dock are all negotiable. I rarely have a musical emergency so acute that I have to access my playlist *right now*.

In short, there is no reason to expect that you will experience serious discomfort by fine-tuning your life and home in these basic ways. We are a tad spoiled by the amount and variety of ways in which to travel, light, and heat our world. Perhaps you will find, as I have, that the best downsizing project you will ever undertake is to limit the decisions surrounding these elemental items in your lifestyle. Develop a code for travel. Plan on lessening your dependence on fossil fuel. Best practices here are better for the future of our planet in a truly fundamental way.

■ Chapter 8

Cleaning: This Ain't Martha's House!

WHEN IT COMES TO HOUSEHOLD CLEANLINESS, I AM DEFINITELY A "GOOD ENOUGH" KIND OF A GAL. Like that biblical Mary, partner of the other Martha, I have better things to do with my mind, my hands, and my time. I was reminded of the rightness of this when I spotted an issue of one of those magazines I read periodically as the modern-day equivalent to self-flagellation, *Martha Stewart Living*. A writer was explaining the death-defying lengths he reached to clean each inch of every window of his high-rise nest. His lyricism on the topic indicated he was thrilled by the risks involved and felt it worthwhile. Hmph! You'll never catch me waxing eloquent about polishing anything!

Let's be clear. My husband and I do not live in squalor. It is safe to accept an invitation to our home. I draw the line at a grubby kitchen. My tub gets scoured. Bothersome thoughts about dust bunnies *under the bed*, however, get banished if the book I am reading *on it* is engrossing.

But there are times when you just have to come to grips with cleaning. Casual I may be, but even I knew that opting for my YBN was not a licence to opt out of basic household maintenance. But how to tackle these chores and still buy nothing? One adapts. One cuts one's coat to suit one's cloth, to use an old-fashioned phrase. And I am old-fashioned when it comes to my domestic habits – and mighty proud of it.

First thing I did was practise a trick that I had already learned from my time with toiletries. I diluted everything with water. You want to curb your carbon emissions? Halve the caustic impact on your septic system? Cut your expenditure on dish soap and liquid hand soaps by 50%? Dilute everything with equal amounts of water. This applies in a different way to laundry products: more about that later.

Although I had retained a few manufactured items from the previous year, I had not stockpiled cleaning products in advance. First, I gave up on most name-brand cleansers long ago when I actually worked for a major manufacturer of cleaning products. Let's just say I know too much. We are victims of our own (carefully nurtured by advertising) need to *overclean* everything in our lives. We do our children no favours whatsoever by subjecting them to a sterile environment in the house only to send their unprepared immune systems out into a grubby, germy world. Increasingly, pediatricians and clinical researchers believe that we may overclean to the peril of the long-term health of our little ones.

I work hard to avoid anything caustic or chemically "floral" in favour of genuinely safe cleaning options. "Safe" means safer for my family and the planet. I have learned not to be bamboozled by the word "natural" on the label of a chemical bomb cleverly marketed as a "green" alternative. "Better for the environment" does not equal *good for the environment*. If you didn't know this already, the rules are basically the same in the nauseatingly fragrant cleaning product aisles as they are at the cosmetic counter. Be skeptical of product claims. In this case, the alternatives are tried-and-true, time-tested tricks. Just clean the same way your grandmother (or her mother) did and the planet will thank you.

My life as an eco-friendly version of Molly Maid is complicated by my allergy to vinegar. As a result, I have to avoid that excellent product in my household, but that doesn't mean you have to. What I've found is that I can get a long way on equal parts hot water, environmentally-safe detergent (products like Down East, Seventh Generation, Dr. Bronner), and elbow grease. That is what I use for most surface cleaning as well as the kitchen sink on a daily basis. When I refer to hot sudsy water in this chapter, I mean a tablespoon of eco-friendly detergent, truly hot water, and rubber gloves. And lots of clean rags and scrub brushes, old toothbrushes and Q-tips as your sidekicks.

Other secrets? My rule of thumb is if I wouldn't eat it, I'm not smearing it on my counter or on any other surface that gets used for food prep. Not that I hanker after the taste combo of lemon juice and baking soda, but you catch my drift. I buy no-name brand lemon juice in large bottles when it goes on special. Baking soda is cheap at the bulk store. Sometimes the sort that is *not* food grade is less expensive and if I see that, I will stock up. The combination is terrific at cleaning stove tops and counters, and works on sinks and tubs, too. It is gently abrasive and, with a slight bleaching effect, it is a less expensive and totally efficacious alternative to harsh cleansers. When I really want to feel good about the sink areas in the house, when guests are coming to stay, I like to make a "paste" from that all-purpose enviro-friendly detergent, full strength, and baking soda, and then grab a toothbrush to get at the difficult area around the taps. (That's also where the Q-tips come in: for the fiddly areas.) Drains that run sluggishly? Try a half-cup of baking soda, followed by a lemon-juice chaser. It will froth up, at which point you urge it back down the drain with a kettle-full of boiling water. It works for me, and that is vital here, where the use of corrosive drain cleaners would be deathly for our septic system, the filtering septic tank, the septic bed, and the water that ultimately drains into the cove where lobsters live and birds nest.

I am also a fan of that little brown bottle of hydrogen peroxide. You may have one lurking in your medicine cabinet. I buy the largest size of 3% solution available at the pharmacy these days, as it is less expensive.

Please note: it is 3% you want. Diluting the 35% hydrogen peroxide is a task best left to professionals; it is too strong to have errant drops flying around.

That friendly brown bottle of 3% may once have been reserved for the maintenance of new ear-piercings and for cleaning cuts, but let it come into its own and be your buddy for household cleaning. It is useful for mild bleaching of everything from teeth to tea cups to tank tops with a stain. It has a multitude of other uses that the Internet is happy to share. My favourites? Cleaning windows and mirrors (no vinegar for me, remember, and lemon juice can leave a residue.) Use it to rinse family toothbrushes in a mild water and HP solution when colds threaten to spread. If you keep up to date on a weekly basis with soap and water and a routine lemon and baking soda cleanse for the toilets, you can pretty much eliminate the need for anything more caustic; simply add half a cup of hydrogen peroxide to the toilet water three or four times a year. Leave for 20 minutes, swish around and flush.

Before we leave the subject of kitchen and bathroom cleaning, I want to add a word about my pet peeve – anti-bacterial sprays. Barring the presence of a seriously impaired immune system in your household, in which case ignore me and seek medical advice, the use of anti-bacterial products is unnecessary. You will end up inhaling the stuff and leaving a chemical residue behind. Unless you routinely strew salmonella-infected raw chicken all over your counter, anti-bacterials just shouldn't be part of your cleaning routine. Hot sudsy water and a good scrub will do the trick. Follow up with a spray of a dilute solution of hydrogen peroxide and water, if you must. The smell of clean is *no* smell, not some floral, catch-in-your-throat spray-on poison.

Now that I have that out of my system, we can move on to the rest of the house. Armed with ragbag, corn broom, feather duster and string mop, I can tackle most of the floor and surface-area jobs. I shamefacedly admit to affection for those Swiffer-style mop-gadgets, but during my YBN (and after) I jettisoned use of the papery-plasticky prefab covers in favour of a gaily coloured collection of my hand-tailored rags, affixed by poking the fabric into the holes. This works just fine at picking up dog hair from the stairs and under the beds, grabbing dust from baseboards, and a quick sweep around after brooming your wooden floors if you live in a sandy spot. After a good shake off the porch, they go back to drag out some more of the hairy hares from under chairs.

My husband, king of the vacuum, does all of the rugs while I sweep and mop wood floors. He is more diligent than I am, even doing the coils under the fridge several times a year, something I managed to ignore for decades. I don't wax floors. (Do they require that with contemporary finishes?) We both like to use a beeswax compound on the pine furniture...seasonally, though, not every week.

We then head out to the compost bin and dump the contents of our vacuum cleaner: apart from the theological allure of dust to dust, human and dog hair (with which our leave-behinds are generously endowed) is a deterrent to the attentions of deer. And that is a big deal where we live. (It also helps to get the men in your family to pee on your rose beds to keep the deer away, but perhaps you don't want to picture that while we are talking purity?) That's pretty much it for keeping our house sanitary in a sane way on a regular basis.

Once a year, we do a turnout of each room, swearing each time that we are moving to a smaller home with fewer rooms. We pull every book off its shelf and dust each one...and pledge to give them to the second-hand bookstore before the next time rolls around. We take down each treasured *tchotchke*, wash or dust it, curse it and vow to sell or give it away and never bother with that item again. We clean the glass on the woodstove, polish the brass (toothpaste and not the micro-bead kind), wash all the windows and get up on stepstools to clean the tops of things, again vowing all the while that we are *never* going to do this again! Then we sit happily admiring our completed work, light a fire as the evening draws in, open a bottle of good wine, and forget all about our resolutions until the next year rolls around.

■ Liberating laundry

I never minded doing "the wash." I go back to the days of the wringer washer, a time before dryers were to be found in the average household. I have done a few loads in my time, but I always enjoyed the process.

My mum and I used to do the weekly washing together when I was a preschooler. We had to go down to the cellar (not a laundry room or even a rec room or basement, but an actual rock-wall cellar!) to do the laundry. It was a dark place: to me, mysterious and alluring. As a small child, I was only ever allowed to go there with my mother, so it remained fascinating. The wringer washer had a big barrel that sloshed hot sudsy water and then cold rinse, with a roller mechanism on top. I passed Mum the wet things in a strictly assigned order, being careful not to drip on the floor. She fed the roller mechanism. When the washing portion was over, we lugged big baskets up to the yard to hang them on the line, me handing things up to my mum one by one. She had pegs in her mouth. In the head portraits I have of my mother, this is one I recall most fondly: hair swept back with a bandanna, out in the sun and laughing as wet shirts flapped back on our faces. This sequence occurred in every sort of weather short of an actual downpour or blizzard. On truly awful days, my mother would drape things indoors on a wooden dowelling affair; I still have one of those.

The best part followed. My father's shirts went on the line, just for a few minutes, then got sprayed with water, rolled in damp towels, and put in the fridge. The next day, my mother set up the ironing board in the living room and got a beer. (It is always summer in this memory.) Then she would iron those shirts, drink her one beer and we would watch *Beat the Clock* on TV. Television was only ever permitted during the day if there was ironing to do.

Then we moved from a flat into a real suburban house. We got a washer. I was promoted to chief pre-sorter. The outdoor hanging still went on, though we had to get a circular rope-cord arrangement on a pole, as our suburb was anti-laundry line. Gentrification took some weird turns in that era. It was another five years and I would have been in my teens before we got a dryer. Even then, it was for towels and "unmentionables" (though I had no such hang-ups! See my remarks on living-better-through-lingerie).

When I first moved from home, there was no laundry equipment in my rooming house. I lugged stuff to a laundromat in a wheelie cart borrowed from an elderly neighbour every second week. I have also used those much-maligned-but-friendly spaces frequently since, especially on vacation or when home equipment breaks down. It is oddly calming to watch your clothes go round and round. There are also collections of exotic reading material in laundromats and you get to meet the nicest people, often with fascinating stories to tell.

When we lived in Italy, we discovered that Europeans are, in their retro-way, further ahead of us in drawing less on the world's resources. Their fuel and electricity costs are far, far higher than ours, so they have learned to conserve. Nowhere is this more apparent than in the laundry room; nowhere does it show up more clearly than in the small-town streets and urban inner courtyards of Italian communities.

Italians do not routinely own dryers. They have laundry machines that are a clever combination of washer and dryer with an extra spin cycle so that for routine loads (you can reduce aggressive spin for delicate) your wash comes out ready to hang. And hanging laundry outdoors is what they do. (Except for underwear: despite in-your-face sexy TV programming with news analysts dressed like cocktail waitresses, Italians can be very modest and every home has their own personal white-metal indoor hanging rack.)

We lived on a *vico*, a small street in a small town. Our apartment on the second floor had two balconies and both had built-in lines ready to accept sheets and towels that flapped high above the heads of the passersby below. Just like in a Sophia Loren movie! Our neighbours all had the same. Lest you think this was limited to the country, you can see hotels, three- and four-star hotels, in Florence and in Rome where the inner courtyards are spider-webbed with clotheslines, awaiting the freshly laundered bed linens of departing guests. Among all the friends we made there, we only knew one who actually owned a standard North American-style dryer and he was an ex-pat who felt properly shamefaced about his purchase and kept it hidden behind a very Italian beaded curtain!

When it came to laundry during my YBN I used the learning of a lifetime and got some new insights, too. I have an HE washer and I use an eco-friendly detergent. I wash in cold water straight from our well except for a monthly white load that I save up. Large loads wash better as clothes wash each other through friction in the machine the way hands do in the sink. Line-drying in the sun does the bleaching for the most part. I got bold in my YBN and cut back on my detergent usage to a half measure of what the manufacturer recommended. The result? Absolutely no discernible difference. Everything passes the sniff test. In truth, it is the *agitation* of modern washers that does the heavy-lifting of cleansing our laundry, *not* the smelly stuff we put in the water.

To eke out my YBN supplies and keep laundry streak-free, I used up the last of my supply and added an occasional half-cup of washing soda (sodium carbonate). This is available through the Arm and Hammer Company, sometimes in the grocery store, and is useful for softening hard (well) water. This product keeps mineral buildup at bay on dark clothes, where deposits might dull colours. I also use Borax (sodium borate – the 20-mule-team variety) for laundry and for many other cleaning uses. Its smaller "grit" size (versus washing soda) means it cleans well in situations where you don't want to deal with the excess of powdery residue created with regular baking soda – inside a refrigerator versus countertops, for example.

Assuming you have purchased for energy efficiency, the best favour you can do to extend the life of your washer is to keep the lid of a top-loading unit or the front door of a front-loading machine *open* all the time it is not in use. This will prevent mildew. This is infinitely preferable to remedying the situation. Some manufacturer instruction books imply that mildew is inevitable and must be routinely treated with cycles of either special caustic cleaning products or full-strength chlorine bleach. Apart from being wasteful and smelly, this is something the water table wants you to avoid. Just leave the door open between rounds and the rubber seal dries naturally.

You don't need me to tell you to clean out the lint trap on the dryer every time you use it. But you may not know that the lint does not need to be immediately binned in the garbage. You can offer it to our feathered friends in spring as nesting material. Pull bird-sized clumps off and strew around the low-hanging branches in your neighbourhood. (Perhaps not when the neighbours are watching; it *does* look a tad unhinged.) Or you can create your own fire kindling. I save toilet paper rolls and those from the inside of wax paper, aluminum foil, or parchment paper, stuff them with dryer lint and add them to the second layer when I start a blaze in our wood stove. Now, I must just add that this is only okay if you do not own a heavily polyester or other plastic-fabric-based wardrobe that you dry in the dryer. This works for cotton lint, wool or bamboo fabric leave-behinds. Don't feed polyester lint to the birds or the air.

And if you want to save 100% of your expenditures on fabric softeners, you can give them up altogether. If you are line-drying versus drying in the dryer, the problem of static cling basically goes away. Towels – in my opinion the one thing that absolutely demands a touch of the roly-poly tumble of the dryer – are the same items on which you truly *must* not use fabric softener. Yes, softeners of either the fluid or "sheet" style may make those towels *feel* fluffy. But the buildup of the waxy chemical ingredient will inhibit the very absorbent qualities that make towels able to dry you off after a shower. And the other chemicals contribute unnecessary pollutants into our environment: among them benzyl acetate, benzyl alcohol, chloroform, and assorted unnatural scents that are toxic (yes, even in the fragrance-free type). The coating will ultimately dull the colour and shorten the life of all your garments and linens. It will also shorten the life of your dryer and can even cause dryer fires that could threaten your home's safety. All this for a fluffiness that is easily achieved by half an hour of line-drying and seven minutes in the dryer. You decide.

Unfortunately, there is no way to make the folding and putting-away part painless. I have a friend with a big family and a separate bin for each member's duds. She just puts the clean clothes unfolded into the appropriate basket and lines them up weekly at the bottom of the stairs. Her results are uneven: some offspring get behind the idea, lug the bin up, dutifully fold and place items in appropriate drawers and return it to the laundry room. But my friend also has a teenager who hasn't gotten into the swing of the thing; she wears the crumpled stuff straight from the pile and often that basket remains at the bottom of the stairs. For the entire week. With everybody tripping over it. You be the judge.

■ They don't build 'em like they used to

An additional word about appliances is in order here. One of the eye-opening aspects of my YBN was how often the need arose to replace existing stuff, particularly appliances. I had taken on the commitment to supply my son-in-law with bread every week and was working my way through that happy task one day in late winter, when my bread machine shook itself into a frenzy while dealing with a particularly daring flaxseed dough, and crashed to the floor. It was absolutely beyond repair.

Naturally, the answer was to revert to mixing, kneading, proofing, and baking bread by hand, which proved rewarding – in the short term. But we all have limitations. Luckily, our family had agreed in advance that any gift-giving opportunities that arose during my YBN would be honoured in a practical manner; my daughter gave me an exact replacement of the fallen machine for my birthday in July.

The dishwasher was another case with an easy solution. It developed a leak and Ronnie, our irreplaceable repair person, advised that, at 10 years of age, my dishwasher fell into the category of "less expensive to replace than to repair." You will have encountered this modern wisdom yourself, no doubt. The parts plus labour (which I could just about defend under the rules of my YBN) added to more than the replacement cost of our basic model. After consulting with my husband, because this situation required his commitment, too, we decided to do all dishes by hand until the end of the year. And we did make a start in that direction. But after some tinkering, the dishwasher came back to a half-life. As long as we were very strategic in our dish placement, we were able to manage without too much dependence on washing by hand. For the record, washing dishes by hand, especially if you repeat the hot-water-suds, clear-water-rinse sink regimen three times daily, uses way more of the planet's precious resources than does the dishwasher.

Then the stove blew up. Black smoke billowed out of the oven on pre-heating. It was only two years old so clearly not up for replacement (although, inevitably, it was two months post-warranty). We were able to repair the oven element and repairs were legal under my YBN rules.

Ronnie and I had a philosophical chat over this one, as he is at the pointy end of the repair-replace debate. He expressed genuine anxiety over how his business has grown. He thinks of the current situation as "manufacturing-assured destruction," the devilish twin of built-in obsolescence. Ronnie believes the customer is not given a fair chance to extend the life of appliances because parts are so rapidly delisted as newer, more expensive models come along. He also says purchasers are given incomplete information to extend the lifespan of their appliances. For example, we are all taught to vacuum the coils on the back of our refrigerators to prevent early burnout. But did you know that those coils are now frequently *under* the machine? Ronnie showed me. How would I have known this and performed the required action without a knowledgeable, sympathetic, and strong ally?

This is the sinister underbelly of modern appliance manufacturing and marketing. The dreadful results are choking our landfills. In an average big-item-disposal-week on our country lane, there are no fewer than five discarded stoves and fridges, though I suspect that some have committed not greater crime than being the wrong colour! White is the new harvest gold as stainless steel becomes the only thing a contemporary kitchen can possibly wear. Or, in Ronnie's version, as the model with the new features comes out, the three-year-old machine not-so-mysteriously develops a glitch, seemingly begging for replacement.

You don't need me to tell you this is a sick system. There are preventative measures we can take instead of adding to the appliance buildup in the landfill.

■ Before you head for the store to buy an appliance, do your homework on longevity through a reliable source, like *Consumer Reports*. Make your expenditure based on this, not the salesperson's spiel or the matchy-matchiness of this new one with your existing units. Trust me: fashion will catch up with your mismatched laundry room. Remember when you had to have shoes and handbag in identical shades? That is *so* 1985!

■ Check out the energy-guide rating of anything you buy new, and buy knowledgeably. When it comes to existing appliances, use them in an energy-wise manner: keep use in check sensibly, cold-water-wash clothes, air-dry dishes in the dishwasher, and hang laundry on the line.

■ Less is likely more: according to Ronnie, the appliance repair guy, the fewer options you have on your washer, dryer, fridge, et al., the less likely it is to go down early for the count. I was appalled when I overheard the real estate pro remark to the owner that the refrigerator in the condo we had been renting would have to be replaced prior to any future possible rental or sale. Why? Because the ice-dispenser didn't work. The refrigerator was in perfect working order other than that. The reason it didn't function? The filter part was no longer available. No potential new resident would even get the option to see if they could live happily without an ice dispenser.

Sigh...

■ Paper and plastic: household alternatives that won't make you crazy and your guests feel queasy

My YBN rules dictated no paper or plastic products. Easier said than done, I found. My kitchen drawers revealed just as many plastic indiscretions as anyone's at the beginning of the year: plastic wrap, three different sizes of freezer bags, and bags left-over from grocery store excursions when I forgot to take my reuseable cloth bags. I used to be very careless with those items, tossing the wrap or bag after a single use. In some jurisdictions, the ability to recycle plastic in a "blue bag" set out curbside encourages people to discard them with a clear conscience. This is flawed logic. There is no recycling remedy that erases the environmental impact of producing unnecessary miles of wrap and millions of bags in the first place.

The bathroom and bedroom paper issues have already been dealt with in a previous chapter, but let me reiterate. We switched successfully to a system of washable cloth hankies and extra washcloths reserved for makeup removal, thus eliminating a constant flow of boxes and paper into our house via grocery shop-ping that would have otherwise swiftly gone back out again in the garbage. (Facial tissue paper, incidentally, has been treated in some way that makes it inadvisable to toss into a septic sys-tem, according to experts. So it's not good to flush "kleenex" down the toilet...does that makes you think twice about putting it up to your face?)

Between handkerchiefs and a square or two of TP every once in a while, most "upstairs" needs are taken care of – we just don't buy that product anymore and, with the exception of small kids with big colds, this works just fine for us. That was a major piece of my YBN learning.

But the kitchen needs a different approach. No paper tow-els, wax paper, or parchment paper refills for me. And *that* was tough. Aluminum foil is mercifully reusable. In fact, if you don't squander it on items with highly acidic exteriors, thus avoiding "pitting," it is practically indestructible. But reusing all those other seemingly indispensable kitchen aids, or giving them up altogether? That was not easy.

I swept the Net for advice. I consulted our daughter and son-in-law, my enviro-warriors. I checked with friends who were ahead of me on this front. And over the course of the year, I developed the following system:

■ In the dishwater, wash and then hang to dry every piece of plastic wrap you come across. I found a two-piece child's garment hanger that worked great for the drying end of this task. I reused those bits of plastic until they were tired right out and shredding. Only then did they get rinsed and retired to the recycling bag. Rarely are they so mucked up beyond salvaging that they have to be thrown in the garbage with the first use.

■ Freezer bags, sandwich bags (baggies), bread bags, and produce bags that you get from the supermarket I treated similarly. (By the way, if you bring fewer of those produce bags into the house, you will have fewer to "save." The cashier really doesn't care if she has to corral an orange or two as long as you place them on the belt in batches – I know, I asked.) I use wooden spoons in a big utensil holder on my counter to hang those bags to dry after washing prior to re-use. I keep a set of attractive baskets tucked into the shelves that hold my cookbooks and more artistic serving pieces. Those baskets hold rags (which I will come to in a minute) and plastic bags of all sizes, ready to hand.

■ Aluminum foil is incredibly durable, bless its shiny finish. Use it, wipe it off, ensure it is dry, fold it and store it, ready to cover leftovers and save cheese (wrap cheese in waxed paper first, though).

■ When it comes to dish covers, here is news your grandmother would happily have shared: use a china or ceramic plate set on a bowl to save many of those items you are accustomed to covering with plastic wrap. I get that a bowl of chopped onions shouldn't be let loose in the fridge, but strawberries? Use a plate to cover while they thaw or macerate or wait to be eaten. I am not a fan of anything plastic going into the microwave, and use plates to cover glass or china items for reheating or microwave cooking as well.

■ In addition to second-hand bread bags et al., the waxy insert in cereal boxes is indispensable for sandwiches going to work or on a picnic. Bring it home again for the next lunchbox.

■ Parchment paper and waxed paper have their uses; they are also compostable, so I am a tad more relaxed about their reuse than some items above. Parchment paper particularly has no substitute for baking, for example, gluten-free peanut butter cookies. (Well, possibly those oven-friendly flexible plastic cookie sheets. I have not tried those, but again, more plastic!) I tried re-using the paper, simply wiping off visible crumbs and arranging the cookies so the second round sat on spaces not occupied by the first round of cookies. It did work, but this is finicky beyond bearing. I should simply bake less to save the world and our waistlines.

Please note: this set of ideas reflects the reality of the very progressive recycling where we live. You may need to adjust for your own system.

You will notice I have not dealt with paper towels. That is because I love the ease of paper towels as an aid in the kitchen. I don't seem to have to deal with those giant messes that TV commercials depend on to illustrate the mop-up abilities of their product. But I *do* lean on paper towels for the following: wrapping herbs for refrigeration, wiping out cast-iron pans, putting on the table instead of cloth napkins when kids and spaghetti are both present at the same meal, and cooking bacon. Now, the first three tasks are just as usefully accomplished with clean, lint-free rags, faded dish-towels, or table napkins – items I stockpile and wash in hot water and hang to dry and sanitize.

But for microwaving bacon, which, in my opinion, is the superior way of cooking it? And then the efficient draining of all visible fat? There simply is no suitable substitute. I confided this dilemma and my unsuccessful attempts at alternatives in a blog entry I wrote around the same time as I was hired on contract as minister at a neighbouring congregation. The wonderful welcoming gift pack I received included a very good history of the church – and a big fat roll of paper towels! Never was a present more warmly welcomed. Now I save my precious paper towels just for bacon and that roll lasts a very long time, indeed.

Housework, a wise person once remarked, expands to fill the time you have to give it. I suspect the same is true of the printed word. Shall we talk about something else?

■ Chapter 9

Entertaining Ourselves to Debt: Making the Most of Leisure Time

I RECALL A TIME, PERHAPS THE MID-1960S AND EARLY '70S, WHEN COMPUTERS WERE NEWLY OCCUPYING THE MINDS OF THE CULTURAL GURUS OF THE DAY. The media was all abuzz about what we would likely be doing with all of our free time in the (then) far-off days of 2001. How would we keep ourselves busy when the work-week had been reduced to three days, the nabobs fretted?

Hmmm, didn't quite work out like that, did it? The number of hours we expend *on* work even if not *at* work is growing by the decade. This growth shows no signs of stopping. There was a time, not so long ago, when I would happily have taken off for a weekend or even two weeks on vacation without dreaming of making arrangements to either keep in touch or be "kept in touch." That simply does not happen today. Instead, we arrange roaming plans for our cellphones before we leave our desk on holidays, whether we go just as a couple or with the kids.

I think that is why leisure time has become such a costly preoccupation. Along with the increase in hours worked came the rise in the complexity and sophistication of leisure activities. The family camping holiday has been replaced by the family cruise or trip to a major theme-park in another province, state, or country. The time may be shorter – three weeks away with Mom and Dad seems a thing of the past – but the five-day winter getaway to an island destination is no longer reserved for honeymoons or retirement bashes. Adventures like skydiving, paragliding and ballooning are no longer the preserve of the super-rich.

Predictably, there has been a backlash and a revitalized interest in diversions like bicycling as a family. After years of condoning conspicuous excess, we again read in women's service journalism of planning a trip to the beach for a picnic as a better way to celebrate a child's birthday than booking an entire bowling alley, bouncy-castle, and clown.

My family have gone to the same place for our vacations for more than 30 years, a camp where there is one telephone, no television or video games or radio, and only one small spot to access WiFi. We eat wonderfully prepared communal meals on benches at big plank tables in an old-fashioned dining room, and we converse. We talk over meals. We chat on the dock as children jump into the dark blue water. We meet for wine and a gossip in wooden chairs strewn over the property. We discuss politics and grandchildren and rock formations and the death of loved ones and kayaks and butterflies with other families and singles and couples that we see only once a year, sometimes never again, and sometimes every chance we get as friendships are forged in the glow of that camp's candlelight.

My mother came with us there for years, accompanied by her best friend. They played Scrabble in the evenings while we read Hardy Boys stories to the children. My daughter and I buried my mother's ashes there. I have asked for the same when my time comes. My grandchildren are already enjoying those holidays. That camp may just be the best thing that ever happened to our family. I wish you a similar experience, with a cottage or a place that is just as special for you. Keep looking until you find it. Or, if you like less predictability and more adventure on your days off, seek *that* and best of luck to you in reinventing the perfect break every single chance you get. Do not ever skip a vacation. They will keep you sane. Just be kind to the planet while you are at it.

Postscript to vacation: that camp that we go to? It is accessible only by car. While we did not have to take a plane, there is no viable combination of train and bus that would have taken our family from here to there, about 800 kilometres. But to limit our environmental impact, we rented a van rather than take two cars. We were four adults, a child and three dogs – in a van, for eight and half hours. Not a pleasure trip you are thinking? What if I told you we went through a hurricane? Worst rain any of us had ever seen and winds that rocked our poor SUV from side to side. Nope, not a pleasure trip. But when we got there we compensated for the lack of fun on the way down by swimming and picking berries and eating lobster on the beach and hiking everywhere, all without depending on a car. It evens out.

■ Entertaining edibles and other free-time frivolities

For my YBN, we decided to clean up our act when it came to dining out. It's so easy, when you are working flat out, to "treat" yourself to a meal out. Soon it ceases to be a treat and becomes the norm. Whether we are talking about fancy dining or stopping at those tempting golden arches with the kids, it adds up. The pounds go on and the money comes out of your bank account with every swipe of that debit card. It is very easy to find yourself eating more meals away than you consume at home if you have lunch at work, takeout on the way to the kids' hockey game, and then meet friends for dinner out on Saturday. But every one of those events uses gas and puts your ability to control your food intake out of reach. You are consuming excess calories, putting money in the greedy paws of corporations and, unless you are tremendously diligent, breaking all the ground rules for careful avoidance of the Dirty Dozen. Fast-food restaurants, Sysco and other restaurant suppliers, chain and otherwise, do not care about your cholesterol, your latent diabetes, or about free-range chickens or grass-fed beef or eating from the Clean Fifteen. They only care about cost. Therefore it is essential that you limit your exposure to the occasional visit to the eateries that get their supplies by the vat.

There are better alternatives. For example, food offerings from places that, generally, are not chains. Find a place that cares about sourcing locally and where you can ask about what you receive on your plate, and get a knowledgeable response. This is often a one-off local establishment. Maybe it is even owned by someone you know personally, if you live in a small town. Even in big cities, however, there are lots of choices for wonderful meals, from the casual bite to seven-course extravaganzas, where the kitchen uses produce and meats that do not come prepackaged off an 18-wheeler.

During my YBN, my husband and I tried very hard to stick to the rules, eating out locally and only once a week (coffee excepted). He was a very good sport about this because it represented a change in our ways – we had become accustomed to buying lunch out when we were at work and, in addition, having two or three dinners out every week. Such an easy habit to get into and, frankly, fun! I really like going out for a meal, trying new places and foods from different countries. When we were first married, we cooked together at home a lot because we could not afford to dine out often. We saved up and maybe went out for a splurge once a month. But over the years that pattern had become a lot more self-indulgent. Cutting way back was something that had to be done.

I was vigilant about supplying lunches for both of us during my YBN. I baked a lot more bread for us. True, I compensated a bit with cookies and pies and fancy puddings at first, but I got stricter as the year went by.

We started to plan and genuinely treasure those meals out. We have a great pub in town that works hard to use local seafood for mussel dishes and fried-haddock plates. And we are blessed with a superb restaurant that is committed to local ingredients and has a very sophisticated menu. Dining out at The Knot Pub and Fleur de Sel became really special events when they were less regularly scheduled. We got further afield, too, and searched out local chowders and clam strips and bakeries and green grocers that offered seasonal items and cared about the source. The bottom line is that we do not eat away from home nearly as much as we once did, and we enjoy it more when we do. Cooking together is starting to be a practice that will enliven our retirement time, too. Especially, as we explore using the produce of our own gardens and the promise of the chickens and the beef cattle that our children are raising.

Having said all that, let me reassure you that I am no angel when it comes to sticking to food rules. There are wicked pleasures in my foodie life. I am not a chain-burger person, but I *do* love an annual fling with fried chicken and, though I have tried to achieve the same effect at home, sometimes I just get a craving for that bucket! Then there's coffee. We spent all that time in Italy where the cappuccino, the expresso, the macchiato, and the café Americano flow like water, only to get off the plane and head straight to our favourite coffee franchise for a double-double. Hey, saints are no fun to live with!

Entertainment is not all about food and vacations: there are pleasures on offer that had implications for my YBN. I had vowed not to buy anything, so we did not go out to a single movie, as that would have cost money and used gas in a way that was not defensible. But we *did* rent and borrow DVDs. I could take a bus to both the library and the amazing source of all things watchable. It is a small, independent rental centre. If you have such a place where you live, go while you still can before they are smothered by online movie streaming services. They have real people who can advise you. ("If you liked *Montalbano*, you will love *Fog and Crimes*.") Librarians can do the same. By sharing DVDs you lessen the impact of the manufacture and individual purchase of reams of plastic.

There is also direct video/digital feed, which involves *no* plastic or other materials, other than whatever already exists in your TV or computer. I hesitate here, because I have a sentimental attachment to DVDs and to the notion of independent local stores and the service they provide, but those are not really environmental arguments, and, to be completely honest, I have already felt the seductive allure of Netflix in my life!

Then there is the music conundrum: records to tapes to CDs to iPods and iTunes and all the variations on that theme. Vinyl has recently made such a comeback that manufacture and sales of turntables are expanding exponentially. It is all too much for this Luddite to keep up with. A useful rule of thumb is to use what you have and wear out all the possibilities before you opt too hastily for a new technology. Remember 8-Track tapes?

As to all other ways to spend your free time, I would just say, please think through the environmental impact of your leisure activities. (Here comes the part where I lose a lot of friends. Sigh.)

It is hard to make an environmental case for most recreational vehicles. Certainly, if you are using a motorcycle rather than a car for travel (as opposed to showing off at the local bar), you are lowering your carbon emissions. But bicycles can be fun, too, even though they don't make that seductive potato-potato-potato noise. (I confess that I am fond of motorcycles.)

But personal watercraft? All-terrain vehicles (ATVs)? Snowmobiles? You are annoying fellow citizens, frightening fish, shorebirds and animals, damaging your own ears with those decibel levels, demolishing shrubs and fledgling trees, and generally adding unnecessary noise pollution and chemical toxins to the atmosphere. Let's all just swim or ski or don snowshoes, instead, shall we?

Golf, once described as "a good walk, spoiled" – attributed variously to Mark Twain and William Gladstone – is much more problematical than that. The demands golf courses put on the environment in terms of upkeep of grounds can be nothing short of appalling. North American golf courses are held to very high standards of maintenance. Keeping those greens and fairways in peak condition requires reliance on synthetic fertilizers, herbicides, insecticides, fungicides, all of which get sluiced off into the water table. Where the water comes from in the first place is another issue. There is sufficient evidence that the water-needs of golf courses can impact negatively the long-term sustainability of all but the most robust aquifers. There are areas of California, for example, a state now notoriously drought-plagued, where it is thought that the existence of so many golf courses has contributed dramatically to the dire conditions.

The news is not all dreadful. In recent years, golf course managers have begun to work with environmental experts to maintain their greens in ways that are less damaging to the environment and human health. Although no accepted standards have yet been established that would qualify a course as "organic" in terms of both products and procedures used, and impact on the watershed, there is little doubt that such innovations are on the way.

In the meantime, let's all clear our heads by going for a long walk. Unless we plan to toss litter as we hike, or shoot something en route, or tear up endangered species for that rock garden back home, chances are this will be an eco-neutral and very enjoyable jaunt.

■ The elephant in your hand: books, magazines, newspapers

Back in 1971, activist Abbie Hoffman wrote a book called *Steal This Book*. This is *not* that book. I am not counterculture or anti-corporate to nearly the same degree as Mr. Hoffman. I truly believe that we, the potential purchasers (I resist describing myself or anyone else as a *consumer*), have far more power than we know to change the way things are made. We can do this by refusing to buy what is on offer. We can then demand what is not currently available. This applies to the purveyor of produce at the local market who never has enough organic strawberries as well as to Procter & Gamble who are perfectly capable of making and marketing less toxic toiletries.

But I am writing a book. And printing books uses paper. Made from trees. Yes, lots of e-books get sold too, but most start life in printed form.

My publisher is *so* not a huge conglomerate. I know that Wood Lake Publishing works diligently to ensure that the people that print the books they choose to publish are as careful as they can be to use safe inks and paper with a decent pedigree;

that those printers believe in reforestation and in turn put their dollars behind efforts to ensure their pulp and paper suppliers are effectively dealing with the inevitable pollution from those processes. Responsibility has a very long tail.

But at the end of the day, this is still a book and I don't want you to steal it. I want you to buy it. I buy books. I love books. The kind with a cover and pages (I will come to e-books later). Then, too, I am mad about magazines. I always have been. Newspapers draw me. The first thing we do when we visit a new place is grab the local papers; language is no barrier to knowledge. You can tell a lot about a town, a city, a nation by what they put in print.

My parents gave me a subscription to *Jack and Jill Magazine* when I was five and just starting to read. It was the beginning of a lifelong love affair with the printed word. I had a roommate once when I was still in my teens, who was horrified that I would spend my summer wages on glossy periodicals (she was an early and deeply committed feminist). "You do know the women in those pages don't actually look like that," she sniffed, disdaining my interest.

Yes, I did know that. Still I was fascinated with the process of getting those images on the page. I loved the juxtaposition of word and picture, the specificity of interest groups served, the smell of the ink and the feel of the ultra-gloss covers. I was excited by the "slap" of my subscription landing on the floor beneath the mail slot in the front hall of my first flat. I was born to work in the publishing industry. When I did work there, I happily turned my nose up at a company car (duh!) or golf club membership as corporate perks, but I would have wept if they had taken away my free magazine subscriptions. Everything from *F1 Racing* to *The New Yorker* to *Quill and Quire* and a zillion niche publications in between.

I really missed magazines during my YBN. The library is good for a quick fix, but you don't get to take them home and read them in bed. You can't turn down the page to remind you to share that article with your spouse. You can't rip out a recipe or book review to save. And, yes, I am aware that you can get most periodicals online these days. It is better for the environment, saving countless trees and the pollution that results from bleaching pulp for paper.

But reading a magazine online is not the same. I still like the feel of the paper stock, the way the magazine spread fills the whole depth and width of my vision and demands the full attention of my eyes and mind. Same with books and with newspapers. For me, there is a tactile element to reading any of those three media that stirs me. My husband, an amateur bookbinder, has taken innumerable courses in that art. He shares my love of print in all its manifestations. We haunt second-hand bookstores and check out the public libraries of every town that we visit. We have never had enough bookshelves in our house to unpack everything – so we rotate our collection. Reading is one of theties that bind our marriage.

While I am adapting to electronic versions of books, online magazines, and digital "print" experiences, I still hanker for the real thing. I lean heavily on libraries for my fixes of magazines. I am both a lender and a borrower of books. There are ways to assuage one's cravings that do not involve going out and buying new. And yet...

Before I come to true confessions, let me pass along the learning that I acquired by doing without some of my favourite things during my YBN. First and foremost, as mentioned, the library was a saving grace. Second, I did ask for a specific book as a gift twice and received it both times. Third, I rationed myself and you can, too.

Even if you can afford it, it just isn't right to have subscriptions to a dozen magazines and to buy every book you fancy. Give yourself a number and stick to it. We have cut our periodical subs from six to one. We only get one newspaper now when previously we had three coming in, one way or another. We rationalize that one as support for the local economy. The books? Well, mostly you can borrow what you want, but I think I am going to set myself an annual book budget of $100 (perhaps five books) for now. This is an important part of my life and I promise to truly appreciate my luck in being able to afford to do this. I also swear to recycle by loaning out anything that is precious, passing on what is valuable to others, and carefully recycling whatever is left over.

■ Relevant confessions

Three times during my YBN I broke the rules. The first time is easily explained away. I'm sure you would have done the same. We went to meet friends at the Halifax habourfront and we took along our young grandson, just short of three years old at the time. Our destination was the Harbour Hopper, an amphibious vehicle tour of the city that was and is the heart's desire of our little guy. It was overcast when we left home and, truthfully, my main concern was whether our adventure would get rained out. Well, Nova Scotians have a saying: "Don't like the weather? Wait 10 minutes!" I should have listened. When it was time for the boat to load, the sun was shining brightly and my husband and I, and worst of all, our little red-haired grandson were all, for once, without hats. And the boat had its canopy open with the sun pouring down. I did what every responsible adult would do in the circumstances and ran to the dock's gift shop and bought the first hat I saw. I felt terrible as I produced my card, but I did what I had to do. The hat is a ball-style cap, turquoise and has a little turtle on it. Our grandchild loves it and is sporting that topper even as I type these words. No regrets.

The other two events both involve the printed word. The first was a totally inadvertent purchase. There I stood, in line at the grocery store, with my organically-correct cartload of produce. My mind wandered to the plight of our young people who were doing a renovation before they moved into their new property. They needed a place nearby to rent short-term. Children and dogs had to be welcomed – not an easy find in our area. I grabbed a local newspaper at the checkout, for them, thinking that there might be something in the classifieds that hadn't made it into Kijiji, country folk being more accustomed to print than online resources. I was out in the parking lot and into the car before I realized what I had done. I was horrified! But when I thought of going back inside and explaining to the cashier, my heart sank. I confessed to my husband, who predictably found the situation hilarious and told me not to even think of going back in. He simply took the newspaper away from me, gave me a looney, told me to forget it ever happened, and dropped that edition of *Lighthouse Now* at the kids' place. Would that all moral indiscretions could be so easily remedied!

The final time I broke my YBN rules, it was deliberate. I bought a book. I bought it for me and my beautiful daughter to curl up on a sofa with, and dream and plan together. The book, by Sara Norrman, is called *Simply Scandinavian*. I blame my sister. She showed me her copy of the book after I had admired for the umpteenth time her home-decorating skills while on a visit. I really like my sister's sense of style, which is something I don't have to nearly the same degree. That pulled-together look? Where you do daring décor things and they look on-purpose, not like some oddball mistake? My sister had, for instance, a child-sized chair affixed to the wall in her entrance way. It looks *so right*. I know if I did that folks would bump their heads on it, curse, and wonder why the heck it wasn't on the floor in the kids' room where it was meant to be. In answer to my questions, my sister showed me this inspired décor book. I loved it! I knew it was just the thing for our daughter (who shares her aunt's knack for dramatic décor touches). I also knew my sister was not going to give up her beloved copy, and I did not ask her. But I wrote down all the particulars before I went home.

When I returned, I went to the library and had the wonderfully friendly and helpful librarian put a search out for the book in our regional system. Nothing doing. I began to scour second-hand bookstores thinking that I could get my husband to make the ultimate purchase, as a mitigating move. No luck. Finally, I looked online. I found it easily. I worried and pondered and told myself that the fantasy in my head, my daughter and me curled up, looking at the pages was not likely anyway. What if she didn't get the *zeitgeist* of the book? Didn't see her farmhouse renovation through the same decorating lenses I did? Finally, I got annoyed with my uncharacteristic dithering. Life is too short for this much angst over a single purchase. I clicked that cart icon and bought a copy.

The book was exactly my daughter's "thing." We did sit together and point out things we liked, or not, and figured out why. We talked about her husband, son, baby-to-be, and all the other children that might come to her some-day home. We made notes and dreams of how she and her family would live and love there in that house, and how her father and I would come for dinner and sit at a table "just like that one." It was a very good purchase and, if I had it to do over again, I would do exactly the same thing.

■ Copper and nickel(s) are precious metals, too: starting small to save big

"If you take care of the pennies, the pounds will take care of themselves." An old-fashioned phrase, still true despite references to out-of-date and foreign coinage. Hang on to your nickels and you will have fewer problems managing the dollars. If there is an economic (as opposed to environmental or ethical) lesson to be learned from my YBN, that is it right there. One of the first questions I am asked now that the year is over is "How much did you save?" Sometimes questioners blurt it out and then physically draw back as if they have mentioned something inappropriate. But I think it is a very good question. I could couch the answer in these terms: I saved money while saving myself. I could even urge others to try a YBN using that most seductive of blandishments: save money while saving the earth!

I did not undertake my YBN as a dollar-saving measure. That is just one of the happy consequences of keeping my hands off my wallet. For the mathematically minded, the net impact is a savings of approximately 15% to 21% versus our average annual household expenditures. For the downright persnickety, the range is offered because we opted out of that vacation to France. The cost would have represented an outlay over the average. Not a holiday that would be part of our usual annual plan, though we could have swung it. But as I've already said, we decided against it in tribute to the ethos of my YBN.

So where did I tally the biggest savings? Oddly enough, the single largest item appeared in previous year's budgets as "walking around money." In the past, I routinely withdrew $50 every week and proceeded to blow it on…apparently nothing very much at all. I was oblivious during my YBN to the lack of walking-around money, but I still walked around.

Apparently, for some time I have been flinging cash at chocolate bars, nail polish, fancy soaps, and impulse "gift" items, like a crystal bear for my little grandson on Valentine's Day. He loved bears and was fascinated by the prisms of crystal objects, so my pre-YBN thinking would have been, "Why not?"

I have a fresh way of evaluating purchases now and this item would never have passed those new standards. He was two and had no idea what Valentine's Day was about. (I wish he never had to know; I am all for romance, but this made-up holiday is an excuse to spend money on things that are healthy neither for our planet nor our personal well-being!) That little bear might have broken and the glass cut him. The trinket was made in some far-off place and travelled a great distance to get to that store, polluting and emitting carbon all the way.

A portion of that walking around money would previously have been spent on transportation. I still purchased bus tickets since "walking around" translated into "busing around" on occasion, and I mentioned already that I did take taxis a couple of times. But not a couple of times a week, as I once did. Basically, what it came down to is that I didn't spent $2,000 and I didn't even notice.

Not purchasing clothing, shoes, and beauty products and limiting hair-salon visits added another $1,500 to the savings. Admittedly, I was the recipient of thoughtful gifts from friends and family of manicures and beauty products, but not nearly to the level of impulse buying I indulged in formerly. No longer will my toiletry drawer hide 50 ways to gloss my lips.

What I hankered for most was my monthly assignation with the magazine rack. "No books" (with that one exception) was easy as I renewed my love affair with the local library. But printers' ink courses through my veins as I have just confessed. Cold turkey on periodicals was *killer*. I bullied my husband into picking up *F1 Racing*. *Vogue*'s September issue kept making eye-contact with me at the supermarket checkout. I wept when my daughter cancelled her subscription to *House and Home*, denying me my fix of domestic décor lust. (I might be lousy at decorating, but I sure love gazing at examples of it done right.) I stopped just short of haunting waiting rooms and gorging on ancient copies of *Reader's Digest*. But I did save $1,000 on books and magazines and newspapers overall. And our beloved *New Yorker* still arrived each week thanks to my husband's timely renewal. I didn't want the subscription on my marriage to run out...

Eking out my craft supplies and raiding the kitchen for gift-giving was actually good fun. Baking bread and making candy, canning jelly and embroidering pillowcases, knitting scarves and painting: all this yielded savings of nearly $1,000. It is very easy to justify buying something on impulse for someone else that you might never buy for yourself, isn't it? A silk pillow cover for your friend's new sofa, or that electric deck-washer for your spouse can really drive up expenditures in this area.

Our bottom line improved markedly. Admittedly, the early days of the following year *did* show some catch-up buying. I bought new face cream, for example, but not the toxic brand I previously used. Instead, I indulged in a Weleda wild rose-scented cream that is just as soothing for both complexion and olfactory needs. I did get a new serviceable-for-church navy (not black) coat. I came nowhere near, however, to reinvesting what I had previously saved, not even by a quarter. It is safe to say that I am not as inclined to impulse buying as I once was. We carefully think through major household purchases and I pause before even small additions these days. These are the questions I ask myself today:

- Do we really need to buy this item? Now? Or can we service/paint/renew the old item? Better yet, can we do without?
- Is there an alternative that is better for the environment?
- Could we rent or borrow this, rather than purchase it?
- If we do buy this, can we share it with others? This is especially important for larger items, like a log-splitter. Think about sharing things like electric hedge clippers, and ice cream makers... If you use an item less than once a week, could you share it with neighbours or with a family member who lives nearby?
- How will we dispose of this once its usefulness to us is over: recycling, passing along to others, or must it end in a landfill? Is there an alternative that has a more responsible end?

There was a song back in the '80s, a Cyndi Lauper tune, about girls having fun. Well that desire to relax, kick back and have a good time is certainly not gender-specific. At heart, we all want to be happy. We all deserve downtime. If yours, like mine, is enriched by the artefacts and accessories of contemporary culture, by all means use them with pleasure. Just stop and think about the impact of how you take your leisure. There is no need to wantonly despoil nature's realm or to rack up unhealthy debt to participate in the good life.

■ Part IV

Spirit

**(or my best shot at an
environmental catechism)**

■ Chapter 10

The View from Here

IT WAS FROM THEOLOGIAN, AUTHOR, AND ACTIVIST MARY JO LEDDY'S OWN LIPS THAT I FIRST HEARD THIS STORY. It may be an exaggeration to say that it changed the path of my life, because that road had already forked for me. I was enrolled in theological studies. The story did, however, move me greatly and has influenced my thinking ever since. I encountered the tale again in Mary Jo's book *Radical Gratitude*. I commend it to all with a heart beating in faith.

Leddy was sitting at the kitchen table in Romero House one day, when a young female resident joined her. Romero House is a shelter for refugees founded in 1992. When invited there, regardless of their faith, those who pass through the house are treated as brothers and sisters, worthy of respect in the resettling process. They become family to the staff and interns, who follow the vision of this charitable foundation named in honour of Archbishop Oscar Romero of El Salvador, who was martyred for his outspoken defence of human rights.

All stories, well told, become the property of the listener as soon as they are heard. So it is with this one and in my mind it is a sunny day and the two are sharing a cup of tea while enjoying a view of the yard.

Finally, from her limited English, the young woman finds the words to shape the question: "Who lives there?" she asks, pointing out the window.

Mary Jo's eyes follow the woman's gaze. "Oh, that is a garage."

"But who lives there?" the young woman persists.

"Well...*no one* lives there," says Mary Jo, her words slowing, as she attempts to explain. "It is a house...for a car."

The woman stares, her eyes going from Mary Jo to the garage and back, in total disbelief.

* * *

WE TAKE FOR GRANTED SO MUCH IN OUR SOCIETY — SO MUCH THAT IS DENIED TO SO MANY PEOPLE IN THE WORLD. How absurd it seems, outside the context of our own narrow interests, to build a sturdy, weatherproof structure — often with windows and large enough to shelter a family — *for a vehicle.*

When I set out to undertake my YBN, I did not think of it strictly in spiritual or religious terms. It began as a simple New Year's resolution — stop adding to the stuff in my life and avoid personal abuse of the resources of our shared earth. But the pledge grew and became part of a journey of faith for me. Whenever I felt that little pinprick of sacrifice at having to put back the cute pink T-shirt, or the latest Lee Child paperback, I was reminded that part of my charge, either as minister or as laity, is stewardship of the planet. In The United Church of Canada, the *New Creed* urges us "to live with respect in creation." Buying adorable paper cocktail napkins with witty sayings is just not part of the deal.

Christianity is a sturdy faith — the Aberdonian Scots Presbyterian version that I was tutored in as a child is a serviceable system of beliefs that was most useful in a century that swung between peace and war like an overwound pendulum. Though it continues on and remains deeply useful for many, it is *not* my version of faith now. I joined The United Church of Canada before I was married, after church-testing for a couple of years. The UCC encourages questions on all topics of faith. I love that about it, though I know some people find the lack of absolute answers frustrating. UCC theology is broad-minded enough not to claim exclusivity. It holds that there are many paths to the Divine, and thus encourages respect for the faiths of others and for those without faith. Theologically, this is a comfortable position for me.

I don't think it matters if you believe as I do, or whether your path to the Divine is different from mine, though I hope you do have *some path*, or are searching. Of course, there are dark days when I am not sure whether Christianity can make any valid claims at all, never mind exclusive ones. But I have more bright moments than dark moments – bright moments when I am certain that this world is *not* by accident, that this life has meaning beyond our ability to acquire things, and that the solidarity of people of faith, of all stripes, will help to ensure the survival of our planet.

What I do know for sure is that people who belong to a family of faith have both the means and a reason to secure the future for the peoples of this earth. Certainly those who do not believe in God or Ganesh, or follow the teachings of Jesus, or Muhammad, or Buddha or Zoroaster can and absolutely *must* claim a stake in saving the planet. There is, after all, plenty of work for all to do. But people of faith who believe that there is some meaning to life and some purpose to this planet beyond its ability to feed and warm us, are dually blessed and burdened with a responsibility to preserve the gift we have been given.

In March of my YBN, when I saw a notice for a Lenten service at a neighbouring church, it struck me that my YBN was like an extended Lent. I had given up something but the point was not that I give up something simply for the sake of giving it up, or that I suffer endlessly. (Which is a good thing because, as I trust this book makes clear, I *didn't* – suffer endlessly, that is.) The point was that my decision to "refrain from buying" reminded me of how casually I have enjoyed the privileges that go along with this life. Like that house – for a car.

When did life get to be like this? When did we shift from homes with four children and one bathroom to homes with one child and four bathrooms? I know that there is something about the relentless thrust of upward mobility that spawns a need for "more," but at some point surely we need to cry, "Halt! Enough!" Recently, I heard about some 10,000-square-foot houses for sale. These are not mansions reserved for some crazy-rich, celebrity-movie-star-athlete, but houses constructed for a suburban development just outside the city of Chicago. Can you imagine what it will cost the earth in fossil fuel to heat a house of that size in that cold, cold place? Have we all gone mad?

But you can only rant at others if your life is above contempt. Here I put myself in the position of Caesar's wife, needing to be above suspicion, yet, environmentally speaking, I am no such thing. On my public blog and in my personal life, my YBN sparked questions.

Wasn't I showing off? That, to me, was a bit of the tall-poppy syndrome taking root. I hadn't set out with the idea in mind to write a blog, much less a book. But I was encouraged to do so and I am sanguine about the publicity involved. If people want to take issue with the fact that I undertook this year and then posted, wrote, and spoke about it, so be it. I am not going to apologize for taking the time to share my experience.

Disapproval was also expressed because I was *deliberately* denying myself what might be considered frivolous items, a buying pattern that I could catch up with as soon as the year was over. Some people pointed out that some of my unmade purchases would have represented untold luxury to a person living in poverty. I could apologize for having been born healthy and ambitious and lucky. For being publisher of *Chatelaine* and for being granted the gift of the gab. Would the gesture represented by my YBN have been nobler had I been poor and unknown? I don't know, but I trust that I have at least partly succeeded in turning the small notoriety of my life to advantage in a good cause. That's what I hope, and it's the best I can do.

■ What I did while I wasn't buying

Believe this: you would have time on your hands if you gave up buying stuff. It takes hours out of your life to acquire things. Sit down right now and look at the past month of your life. How much time might be gifted back to you if you weren't driving to a store, strolling down a street window-shopping, or struggling through a mall on a Saturday afternoon trying to find the perfect _____ (shoes, chair, lawn ornament, Christmas present, wallpaper – you fill in the blank).

Shopping takes up enormous amounts of our time. We go with a friend and make it a social event. We devote an entire day to doing retail chores with a spouse. We teach our children by example and then wonder why they bug us for a larger allowance, their own credit card, and seem obsessed by material possessions.

When you have figured out how much time you spent buying stuff, think how you might have spent that time instead. I used my new-found time in various ways, but there is one day that became iconic for me.

There are high-water marks in every collector's life. During my YBN, a period of low tides was actually the high-water mark time for me, for I collect sea glass.

I met my paternal grandparents only once. I have shared already how much influence a chance visit to a train station with Gwa had on me. But I have a legacy beyond that. My grandparents took me to visit the sea near where they lived in England. Strolling a Bournemouth beach, Nana Katy bent to retrieve a glass pebble. Slipping it into my 4-year-old palm, she told me about "mermaid tears."

Neptune, so the story goes, that bully god of the oceans, forbade willful mermaids from exercising their powers to change nature's course without his explicit say-so. One sea-maid adored from afar the handsome ship's captain who traversed her watery territory. When his vessel started to falter in a wintry storm, her beloved was left clinging for life to the wheel of his ship. Our wayward mermaid defied Neptune and calmed the waves, permitting the brave captain to save his ship. Neptune was furious and banished the sobbing mermaid to the depths. To this day, so the tale goes, her tears wash up on the shores of the world as sea glass.

I save my bits of legend in multi-coloured layers in a high glass jar, a parting gift from my brother-in-law, Michael. He kept his matchbook collection in it. He passed it on with instructions to fill it to the brim with my glass bits, and to not even think of giving up this life until I had a complete layer of blue. Sea glass comes in various hues, from the commonest brown, green, and clear (think beer bottles), to the much rarer indigo and aquamarine. Shards of red, "black," and orange are hardly found at all. I have a mere handful of those colours and will bequeath the completion of that layer as a quest for my grandchildren.

It was Easter Monday of my YBN when I had my best sea-glass day ever. The laundry on the line reminded me of the weekend's feasts. My great-aunt's pink linen tablecloth and a tea towel, stained yellow with the turmeric my daughter and I had used to dye Easter eggs, flapped there in the spring breezes. I hung these early so we could head for the beach with the dogs before that extraordinarily low tide came sweeping back to mask the sands again. The yield of smoothly sand-polished glass is best then, revealing nuggets of crystalline colour that would otherwise remain forever hidden.

That day, the unthinkable happened and my husband, our grandson, and I found *three* blue bits. As with all collections, identifying provenance is the charm. This particular shade of blue was reminiscent of bottles of German white wine and, also, the jars of the eucalyptus-scented face cream my mother used.

That same singular English summer, when I first heard the story of the mermaid's tears, my grandfather took me around his tiny garden and tutored my nose. Do you know every rose varietal has a different scent? This lesson, love of train travel, some faded photos, and the mermaid's tale are all that remain to me of these two wonderful people. But those memories fostered a lifetime of pleasure for me and mine.

How blessed I am that it was *something of themselves* they proffered and not merely something they purchased. I have taken this lesson to heart. Whatever time God gives me with our grandchildren I spend reading, cooking, painting, picnicking, swimming, hiking and talking. I want to bequeath to them only the best of what I have learned. It is my soul's delight that our beautiful daughter and her wonderful husband allow their children to attend the church where I preach. I am saddened when I hear young couples say they intend for their children to decide for themselves about church and then use that to justify never bringing them inside the door of a synagogue, mosque or chapel, as if a deep ignorance and mistrust could ever inform choice!

If I could give those little ones faith, I would, for I truly believe it is the greatest gift of all, nourishing as it does a sense of wonder, gratitude, and hope. Without that hope and the sense of optimism it fuels, I know I would not have the courage to fight against the relentless materialism of this society. For me, both hope and optimism are fed by my faith in this world and its inhabitants, *as manifestations of the Divine*. That is what makes any amount of effort to cleanse this world and ensure quality of life for all generations worthwhile.

■ The time I discovered true abundance...

There are three things that are essential to life: water, nourishment and a warm shelter. Here in Canada, we are truly blessed in that all three are relatively accessible to all. Of course, there are the bigger issues of how pure the water is, what kind of food is available, what sort of shelter are we talking about, and how is it heated. I have dealt with the practical elements of these issues earlier in this book, but I'd like to set them in a slightly more spiritual context here.

I am acutely conscious now that we have a duty to listen to author Michael Pollan's wise insight: "We are what we eat, it is often said but of course that is only part of the story. We are what we eat eats too."

We must pay attention to what is consumed by the animals we consume. We must understand the soil in which our wheat and our vegetables grow. We must know what flows into the waterways we tap.

It is imperative that we support a saner approach to diversified land use than the big-business farm models that are literally poisoning our earth. If we don't feed good things to our cows, how can we expect them to be good for us to eat? True abundance is about having cow's milk be a pure product from a well-nourished animal. True plenitude is not about the luxury of eating every vegetable from every place all year round, but about eating an excellent example of a locally-grown beet, for example, in its own season in our own town.

Truly, when it comes right down to it, it is all about taking care of our earth.

The need to "take care," to practise "stewardship," was brought home to us during the summer of my YBN, when the storm hit. Hurricane Arthur roared through our region early that summer with an enormous appetite for frail and failing trees. Our property is large enough that the six it brought down and the three dozen it revealed as weak hardly made a rent in *the shade canopy.* That's how we referred previously to the wildly overgrown mess of unkempt greenery we'd been ignoring for a decade. We have since tamed that mysterious wilderness and have started to know our trees. The result will be a managed woodlot in the years to come. Our goal now is a sustainable future for this piece of God's earth.

It is our intention to heat our designed-to-purpose home solely using wood fuel, leaving only a small amount of fossil fuel (oil) in the tank to keep the water heater going. There is much debate in books and online about whether it is less ecologically harmful to burn oil or wood. I've explored some of that here. For rural folks with no near neighbours, a clean chimney and up-to-code wood stove, the jury comes down firmly on the side of burning properly aged chunks of hardwood from your own land.

Green wood, that is a recently cut tree, does not burn cleanly. However, we already had a sufficient supply of dry hardwood for my YBN. We took the newly fallen as contributions for future woodsheds. A crew of local young people, those who have not departed for Alberta, felled 43 trees on our acreage over three weekends. They all have other work, but salaries for those who remain on the coast are not luxurious. Most must work two jobs. Their earnings included the trees we could not use – enough, we figured, to fuel six or seven other households. The crew left us three trees of various thicknesses to split and stack. My husband is a self-taught splitter and has become adept at judging how much of the "crop" to chop skinny, for quick kindling; how much to leave intact for long slow nighttime burns; and how much to cut as daytime medium-burning chunks. They all must age before they can join the woodshed logs, as those are the ones that get burned first.

I am the stacker of those pre-woodshed portions. Now, woodpile stacking is an art in these parts and I do not pretend that my feeble attempts to create some kind of symmetry compete with the artistry I frequently see around me. At first, I was intent on "getting 'er done," as they say. The first lesson was settling the logs into a stable position that prevented them from toppling onto my feet. ("Oh, so *this* is why country people do not sport sexy sandals in their sunny gardens in August!")

As the hours of rhythmic log placement wore on, I ceased to be aimless and gradually came to understand both the practicality and artistry of the woodpile stacking plan. Some favour great beehives and others pyramids. Some go for rows of symmetrically placed wooden mosaic. My efforts are pathetic compared to the pure poetry of my neighbour, Nellie, who in her mid-70s still axe-splits her own annual wood fuel.

But what's really important here is that with every heft and every cautious placement of every log, I was aware of the gifts of nature. I knew I was honouring the earth, both by removing what needed to be used and by leaving behind enough to nourish the forest. That's what stewardship of the earth is about, and it applies to all the resources of the earth, not just to trees and forests.

I also discovered a new definition of plenitude. True abundance is enough money in the bank to fend off debt, enough preserved goods put by to prevent hunger in a blizzard, and enough wood to keep you warm all winter. To my *new* way of thinking, abundance is having *just enough*.

My former lifestyle was as environmentally damaging as the next man's or woman's. And now it is less so…by what? Maybe five percent? It may not be much. I have cleaned up my cleaning act. I buy less, and more responsibly. I hope that this will cause fewer items to be wastefully produced and wantonly shipped. We eat a diet that is less threatening to our family and the planet. We support those who are working toward sustainable farm development.

That's it. Is it enough? I don't know. But *God* knows, and I can follow that plan of faith and hard work as generations have done before me.

■ Conclusion

What about that Economy?

HERE'S A QUESTION I HEARD OVER AND OVER: "IF WE ALL DID WHAT YOU ARE DOING, WOULDN'T THE ECONOMY COLLAPSE?"

Yes! It might topple, which I think would be pretty darn terrific since I believe this economy could afford to fall, only to rise again a little leaner and straighter. Maybe I am more like Abbie Hoffman than I claimed earlier. However, this is not really a genuine concern since we are *not* all going to do this for a year, a month, or even a week, are we? But we could try a day, couldn't we? Just to establish that we are indeed still *citizens*, not just *consumers*.

I was going to end this book with a review of various economic theories. I am not going to do that after all, for reasons both frank and cowardly. First, and perhaps most importantly, because I am no economist. As someone with both a business and a theological background, I see too much chaos in the world to trust any tidy summation of those mysteries.

But like I said, it was originally my idea to review whatever theories were most topical and see how they applied to my YBN. The book *Capital in the Twenty-First Century*, by the academic Thomas Piketty, was very much being discussed when I set down my plan. Then I saw so many expert opinions proposed and rejected on the importance of that mammoth study of economic inequality. What clarification could I possibly bring? If you have the time and the arm muscles for it, by all means get hold of a copy. You might also like to read a controversial review/rebuttal by writer Stephanie Flanders in the UK's *The Guardian* newspaper. Then you can enlighten me.

I also heard divergent perspectives on the real-life workability of the "sharing economy." Yes, at its best, for example with car sharing, this model of collaborative consumption has a right to its claim as being both ethical and economically viable. However, sharing-economy definitions also shelter both eBay and Airbnb, both of which I find somewhat suspect – not as they first started out, but in the giant sales machines they have become. Can the sharing economy contribute to environmental sustainability if it does not discourage proliferation of stuff?

Is there an economic model that proposes that we all simply consume less? I don't know. But that is what it is going to take. Is there a system that encompasses the wisdom of "use it up, wear it out, make it do, or do without"? *Doing without* is such an anti-capitalist position to endorse for a generation brought up, as mine was, to think always of progress as a good thing. I heard Canadian Green Party politician Elizabeth May (who I admire immensely both for her brain-power and her ethical stance) speak recently. She quoted Ed Begley, Jr., American actor-turned-activist: "When we destroy something created by man we call it vandalism, but when we destroy something [created] by nature we call it progress." I share that mistrust now, though admittedly I am late to the party.

Because of an early education rooted in the moral good of upward mobility, I was inclined to feel depressed at first as sources as diverse as the *Pew Research Center* and *Business Insider* insisted that our offspring are going to be less financially well-off than we are. Specifically, the studies suggest that those born after 1970 hold wealth that, when adjusted for inflation, is well below what we – meaning those of my generation, the boomers – held when we were the same age.

At first blush, this invoked a feeling of sadness and even guilt in me. But is that initial reaction warranted? What good did all those hard-earned wages, that inherited money, and that wealth acquired through inflated investments do for the world? It is not as if the benefits were equally distributed. On that I *do* agree with Piketty's premise: there is an increasing gap between the 1% of society that is very rich and growing richer daily, and the world's disenfranchised and impoverished.

What good have we, the boomers, done for the earth? That is the study *I* would like to read. The one in defence of a generation of idealists who had good intentions of freeing themselves from the fetters of conventional greed. How did those hands across the world become hands that made the biggest cash grab in a single generation – ever. And we crapped all over the planet while doing so. I don't think it would be easy to write that treatise.

Surely there is still time to reverse history's likely take on our demographic? I truly believe that we can take back our pride in being boomers by living out the rest of our days well, and by giving back wisely and generously. If I were endowed with the money of a Bill and Melinda Gates, I would do as they do and give vast amounts away. If you have read this far, and if you had the same amount of money, I suspect that you would do the same. Your personal philanthropy, however, may well, like mine, be measured in hundreds, not millions, of dollars.

My theory is that we can contribute to the future by *using* less. Yes, by all means give money to good causes. But also give more things away. Give up your time to do something helpful. Give up your need to have the latest, the shiniest, the matching, the unnecessary addition to your collection of *whatever*, in favour of the *essential*.

That's it. That's the end of the rant!

Back to the primary question: Are you a traitor to "the economy" if you undertake a year a month, a week, or a day of buying nothing? If we all gave up buying something new from retail sources for a period of time, would this have a serious negative impact on the economy? Again, as is clear, I am no economist. But I *do* know that the human mind is infinitely inventive. So let me fantasize.

Take, as an example, one of my particular pet peeves: that perceived need for a matchy-matchy set of kitchen appliances. At the moment, we succumb to the dictates of the magazines (which I, admittedly, love to gaze at) and the television programs that tell us that anything less than a burnished stainless steel stove, fridge, and dishwasher combination will make your kitchen appear dated, unattractive and, if you've a mind to sell it, unsaleable.

Under the current system, you might be encouraged to ditch the appliances you already have and buy three new items. You are certainly discouraged already from reviving your existing appliances because of a lack of useful replacement parts and, possibly, ever-decreasing options in terms of people who can service them. Plus, you tell yourself that you are creating jobs by buying new items.

The chances are, however, that those appliances are currently made in some far-off place, and that the profits from the sale do not provide much positive effect locally. The jobs impacted by your purchase of a new refrigerator may be limited to a very few pay packets: teamsters who unload them at the harbour, the truckers who bring them to the store, and the salesperson who sells it to you. Well, it's a start, I suppose. Maybe ten or 15 local or national pay packets slightly impacted by each sale?

What if, instead of being hell-bent on buying new, you refused and instead sought out a method of salvaging your existing set? Of replacing any defective parts and then renewing the appearance of your existing set of appliances? Just recently, I chatted with a local carpenter who is patenting a method of cladding appliances in a veneer of salvaged wood. What if his environmentally sound idea grew and became the norm in communities around North America? What if that was what got celebrated in décor magazines and on TV as the latest trend? What if we then exported this cladding system and the expertise to those faraway places? What if all this yielded jobs, in replacement-part manufacturing, wood salvage, cladding and installation? Not just a dollar or two of commission added to a statement of earnings, but whole jobs created?

Now I know that for everyone who gets my point there are five who are thinking up reasons why my fantasy scenario can't work. That's fine. Make up your own *better idea*. In my example, we would be wresting back control of some elements of our own future. If we stop buying the thing that is not good for us, for our planet, for our local or national economy, smart minds will find a way to rush in with a homemade, profitable, less-damaging equivalent. Nothing may abhor a vacuum more than Mother Nature, but the brain of an inventive entrepreneur can be a fertile place.

We, the potential purchasers, must create the need. If we go on buying the big shiny appliance sets, with no regard to their provenance, or to what has been dumped where to make room for them, then we have no need for healthier, more local solutions.

So if you go without buying something for a year, a month, a week, or a day, especially if you let others know about your self-restraint, you are sending a signal that you expect and will demand, innovation. And you just might inspire change. That change *can* and *should* be more beneficial to the planet *and* to our own economic future than the status quo. And little by little, by buying *nothing*, we will have created *something* better. A better world for us and for our children and our children's children ... all we ever wanted.

The Long View
An Elderwoman's Book of Wisdom
Donna Sinclair

This book is about finding and offering hope. It's about claiming the full meaning of eldership and knowing that elderwomen have much to offer. The collection of 365 daily reflections offers elderwomen an opportunity to nourish the wisdom and deep knowing that comes from life experience. It also holds out the potential for growth, the opportunity to waken to different perspectives that can lead to rich possibilities and courageous actions.

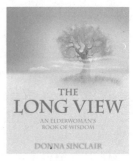

This is territory Donna Sinclair knows well. Retired from a 35-year career as a respected journalist, Donna has found plenty of life and purpose to carry her forward. In particular, she has come to realize the important role elderwomen can play in our society – remembering the past, speaking out against injustice, seeking to restore the balance of creation.

Donna also knows that in order to accomplish these difficult yet essential tasks, elderwomen need to nourish their inner life.

A journalist for more than 30 years, Donna Sinclair is an award-winning writer who has travelled widely in Canada, Africa, Central America, Britain, and Eastern Europe. She is the author of *The Spirituality of Bread*, *The Spirituality of Gardening*, *A Woman's Book of Days*, and numerous other titles. Donna lives with her husband, Jim, in North Bay, Ontario.

336 PP | 6" x 7" | Paper
$19.95 | ISBN 978-1-55145-595-2

Creative Aging

Stories from the Pages of the Journal
Sage-ing with Creative Spirit, Grace and Gratitude
Karen Close & Carolyn Cowan, eds.

Creative Aging is a powerful new social and cultural movement that is stirring the imaginations of communities and people everywhere. Often called Sage-ing, it takes many forms: academic, social and personal. Sage-ing is about seeking - satisfying inner gnawing and transforming it to knowing and action. The creative journey into self is a strong aid to health and wellbeing for the individual and to our culture. *Creative Aging* brings together more than 50 essays and galleries of images that showcase the power of the imagination expressed and enjoyed.

KAREN CLOSE is a painter and author of two books. *Unfinished Women: Seeds From My Friendship With Reva Brooks* chronicles Close's friendship with aging Canadian photographer Reva Brooks. Spirit of Kelowna: A Celebration of Art and Community profiles a community art project. Teaching English and Visual Arts for 27 years gave Karen a deep appreciation for the healing benefits of creative expression. In 2011 Karen created the online journal *Sage-ing* to expand awareness of creative aging.

CAROLYN COWAN is a student of poetry and likes to paint in her spare time. She's a regular volunteer with Hospice House in Kelowna. Although Carolyn lived abroad and in Toronto for many years, the West with its prairies and mountains are in her bones.

320 PP | 6" x 9" | Paper
$24.95 | ISBN 978-1-77064-790-9

Wood Lake

Imagining, living and telling the faith story.

WOOD LAKE IS THE FAITH STORY COMPANY. It has told:

• The story of the seasons of the earth, the people of God, and the place and purpose of faith in the world

• The story of the faith journey, from birth to death

• The story of Jesus and the churches that carry his message.

Wood Lake has been telling stories for more than 30 years. During that time, it has given form and substance to the words, songs, pictures and ideas of hundreds of storytellers.

Those stories have taken a multitude of forms – parables, poems, drawings, prayers, epiphanies, songs, books, paintings, hymns, curricula – all driven by a common mission of serving those on the faith journey.